The Sinopedia Series

CHINA'S DIPLOMACY

The Sinopedia Series

CHINA'S DIPLOMACY

ZHANG
QINGMIN

Australia • Brazil • Japan • Korea • Mexico • Singapore • Spain • United Kingdom • United States

CENGAGE
Learning™

China's Diplomacy
Zhang Qingmin

Publishing Director:
 Paul Tan

Editorial Manager:
 Yang Liping

Associate Development Editor:
 Tanmayee Bhatwadekar

Associate Development Editor:
 Joe Ng

Senior Product Director:
 Janet Lim

Product Managers:
 Kevin Joo
 Lee Hong Tan

Assistant Publishing Manager:
 Pauline Lim

Production Executive:
 Cindy Chai

Translator:
 Zhang Qingmin

Copy Editor:
 Angela Dove

Cover Designer:
 Ong Lay Keng

Compositor:
 Integra Software Services,
 Pvt. Ltd.

ISBN-13: 978-981-4319-73-7

ISBN-10: 981-4319-73-2

Cengage Learning Asia Pte Ltd
5 Shenton Way #01-01
UIC Building
Singapore 068808

Cengage Learning is a leading provider of customized learning solutions with office locations around the globe, including Singapore, the United Kingdom, Australia, Mexico, Brazil and Japan. Locate your local office at: **www.cengage.com/global**

Cengage Learning products are represented in Canada by Nelson Education, Ltd.

For product information, visit **www.cengageasia.com**

Printed in Singapore
1 2 3 4 5 12 11 10

Table of Contents

Preface

The year 2009 marks the 60th anniversary of the founding of the People's Republic of China (PRC), and New China's diplomacy has also gone through a journey of 60 years.

The 60-year history of the PRC can be divided into the first 30 years after its founding and the second 30 years since opening up and reform were initiated in 1978. The major diplomatic task of the first 30 years was to oppose the threat from big powers, consolidate national independence, and safeguard sovereignty and territorial integrity. The second 30-year period was dedicated to creating a good international and peripheral environment for its domestic economic development and to promoting China's development in accordance with the changing international situation.

The two 30-year periods of China's diplomatic history have remarkably different features, but are intimately related to each other. The first 30 years scored great achievements in consolidating the state and safeguarding independence. More specifically, the New China had a clear break with the old diplomacy of humiliation; stabilized a new kind of diplomatic relations with other countries on the basis of equality and mutual benefit; secured an equal position and dignity on the global stage; gained diplomatic independence by safeguarding and strengthening national independence, and protecting national security and territorial integrity; settled the border disputes left over from history with most neighbors by peaceful means, creating a stable neighborhood in general; established strong friendships with the vast majority of developing countries through mutual support; and set up a new diplomatic contingent for seeking the diplomacy of independence.

The third plenary session of the 11th Central Committee of the Chinese Communist Party ushered in a new epoch in Chinese history and commenced a new era in terms of China's diplomacy. Holding high the banner of peace and development, China's diplomacy since then has scored new achievements.

First of all, China's diplomacy has created a peaceful international environment for domestic economic development, contributing to a sustained and stable high economic growth, raising China's overall national strength and its international competitiveness. China's gross domestic product (GDP) has climbed from RMB 364.5 billion in 1978 to more than RMB 30 trillion in 2008. China's contribution to world economic growth has surpassed more than 10 percent.

Second, China has been actively integrated into the international community. It has joined more than 100 intergovernmental international organizations, acceded more than 300 international multilateral treaties, participated in 24 UN peacekeeping operations, and dispatched more than 10,000 peacekeeping personnel. All of this makes China an important player on the international stage. While integrating itself into the activities of the international community, China insists on its identity as a developing country and makes its utmost effort to enhance and promote the interests of developing countries according to the principle of balancing between rights and obligations.

Third, China upholds justice in international affairs and has become a responsible power along with its improved international standing. China stands for peaceful negotiation and diplomatic consultation in the settlement of global and regional conflicts, assumes due international responsibilities, and lives up to its commitments in the settlement of such global issues as global climate change and public health. China's proactive policies have been fully recognized by the international community, winning an international image better than ever before.

Fourth, China's diplomatic front has been gradually extended with a good omnidirectional foreign relations structure. Currently China maintains diplomatic relations with 171 countries. In its relations with developed countries, China adheres to the principle of surpassing the differences in social systems and ideologies in order to develop relations with them, seeking common ground while reserving differences. China upholds dialogue while avoiding confrontation, properly manages differences and frictions, expands the areas where bilateral interests meet, and establishes strategic partnerships of various types and cooperative relations with different countries. In conformity with the principle of equal consultation, mutual understanding, and mutual accommodation, China has signed boundary agreements or treaties with 13 of its 14 land neighbors and solved 90 percent of its land border disputes or has reached provisional agreements on those that are still difficult to solve according to the principle of shelving the disputes. These have created a peaceful, stable, cooperative, and win-win peripheral environment on the basis of equality and mutual trust. In relations with other developing countries, China has emphasized its commitment to continuing to enhance solidarity and cooperation with its neighbors. In addition to providing assistance to some of them to the best of its capability, China has increasingly expanded the areas of cooperation according to the principle of "equality and mutual benefit, emphasizing practical results, diversity in forms, and attainment of common development."

Given the new domestic and international situation, China has endeavored to coordinate domestic development and opening up, and has advocated the concept of comprehensive diplomacy: promoting security diplomacy, economic diplomacy, and humanitarian diplomacy. It has developed economic cooperation with all countries, promoted dialogues and communications with other civilizations, and increased the knowledge about and understanding of China by the international community.

China has accumulated a wealth of experience in diplomacy over the past 60 years, realizing that China cannot develop without the world, and the world cannot become prosperous without China. The future and fate of China has been intimately tied with the rest of the world. Whatever changes take place in the international situation, the Chinese government and people will always hold high the banner of peace, development and cooperation; pursue an independent foreign policy of peace; and safeguard China's interests in terms of sovereignty, security, and development.

The Chinese government and people will continue to contribute to regional and global development through its own development, and expand the areas where China's interests meet those of various sides. While securing its own development, China will accommodate the legitimate concerns of other countries, especially other developing countries. The Chinese government and people will increase market access in accordance with internationally recognized economic and trade rules, and protect the rights and interests of their partners in accordance with relevant laws. China will continue to support international efforts to help developing countries enhance their capacity for independent development and improve the lives of their people so as to narrow the North–South gap. The Chinese government and people will continue to support the efforts to improve international trade and financial systems, advance the liberalization and facilitation of trade and investment, and properly resolve economic and trade frictions through consultation and collaboration.

Looking into the future, we believe that China's diplomacy is now at a new starting point. As China becomes stronger with a raised international standing, China's diplomacy is facing greater missions. The burden is heavy and the road is long. What is certain is that China will adhere to the road of peaceful development and that the Chinese people will join the peoples from all other countries to work toward realizing the lofty dreams of human beings.

Chapter 1

Building a Harmonious World of Sustained Peace and Common Prosperity

Unswervingly adhering to the road of peaceful development is the sincere desire and unshakable choice of the Chinese people.

Constructing a harmonious world of sustained peace and common prosperity is the fundamental aspiration and unremitting goal of China's diplomacy.

Giving birth to one of the four great ancient civilizations, China has made marvelous contributions to the world. In developing its relations with peripheral nations and countries over the past centuries, China has formed a China-centered and moral-based harmonious system, which is referred to as the "Chinese World Order."

The Western powers forced open China's door with warships and cannons in the 19th century. In the 100 years after the first Opium War in 1840, China suffered repeated invasions, reducing China to a semicolonial and semifeudal country. Eliminating war and achieving peace, and establishing an independent, rich country where its people could live a happy life have been the assiduous goals for which the Chinese people have struggled in China's recent history.

Led by the Chinese Communist Party (CCP), the Chinese people of different ethnic groups, after a long period of difficult and tortuous struggle, overthrew the rule of imperialism, feudalism, and bureaucratic capitalism, succeeded in new democratic revolution, and founded the People's Republic of China (PRC) in 1949. China's diplomacy opened a new chapter from then on.

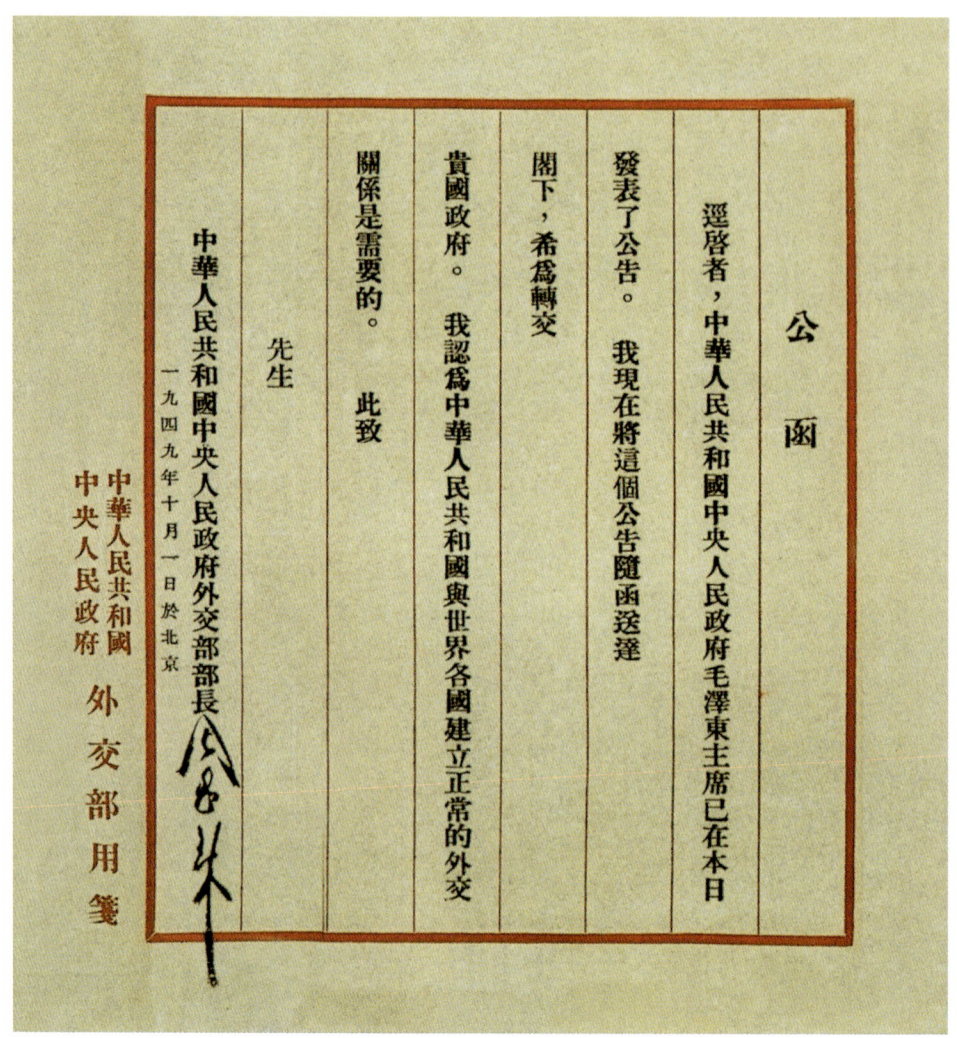

The letter from Chinese Foreign Minister Zhou Enlai to governments of various countries in the world on the proclamation of the Central People's Government, which says China is willing to establish normal diplomatic relations with all countries.

The new Chinese government has held high the banner of peace, development, and cooperation, and insisted on the peaceful foreign policy of independence. The Common Program adopted by the Chinese People's Political Consultative Conference (CPPCC) on September 30, 1949 says: "The principle of the People's Republic of China's foreign policy is protection of the independence, freedom, and integrity of the territory and sovereignty of the country, upholding lasting international peace and the friendly cooperation between peoples of all countries, and opposition to the imperialist policy of aggression and war."

Reaffirming the above provision, the first Constitution of New China enacted in 1954 announces to the world: "On international affairs, our unswerving principle is to work for the holy goal of world peace and human progress." In the past half century, China has consistently been a proponent of peaceful means, and has strongly opposed using or threatening to use military force either in handling its relations with big powers, or in the settlement of past issues with its neighbors, or in the settlement of international disputes or regional hot issues that are not directly related to China's interests.

Since its reform and opening up in 1978, China has, in light of the changes in the international community, grasped peace and development as the two major themes of the present era; persisted on economic development as the core; emphasized that its diplomacy was to create a long-lasting peaceful international and peripheral environment for domestic economic development; held high the banner of peace; stabilized its relations with big powers; cemented friendly cooperation with its neighboring countries; consolidated traditional friendship with other developing countries; actively participated in multilateral diplomacy; and advocated a new international, political, and economic order on the basis of the five principles of peaceful coexistence.

Facing the new international environment, China has continued to strive for a new international political and economic order, promoted the development of multipolarization, and advocated the democratization of international relations and diversification of economic development modes. China has successively put forward its new concepts on security, civilization, and development, as well as the guideline of building a good neighborly relationship and partnership with its neighbors. China has also tried its utmost to coexist peacefully and seek common prosperity with other countries as it develops and strengthens itself.

In his speech to the Asia-Africa Summit held in Jakarta in April 2005, Chinese President Hu Jintao proposed that Asian and African countries should work together to build a harmonious world featuring friendly coexistence of different civilizations, conduct dialogue on an equal footing, and strengthen development and prosperity. In his speech to the United Nations in September the same year, he further elaborated the ideas of "building a harmonious world of sustained peace and common prosperity," revealing a new perspective on world affairs with Chinese characteristics.

The idea of building a harmonious world of sustained peace and common prosperity is a crystallization of earlier Chinese diplomatic thoughts. It emphasizes coordination of interests of different parties and resolving conflicts that may exist among them, seeking win-win results to further their utmost interests, and to gain win-win goals through peaceful and cooperative means, given that

People in Beijing mark the International Peace Day on the Great Wall on September 21, 1999.

diversity, conflicts of interest, and the coexistence of different civilizations are the reality of the world. The idea of "building a harmonious world" is also a demonstration of the peace-loving elements in Chinese traditional culture. The concept of a harmonious world complies with the spirit of the UN Charter and the domestic policies of China, embodying the unity of China's peaceful development and the world's stability and prosperity as well as the unity of the fundamental interests of both the Chinese people and the people throughout the world.

Building a harmonious world of sustained peace and common prosperity is the lofty goal of China on its road toward peaceful development. China holds that a harmonious world should be democratic, friendly, fair, and tolerant. To reach this goal, China advocates the following four principles:

1. Upholding democracy and equality to achieve coordination and cooperation. All countries should, on the basis of the UN Charter and the Five Principles of Peaceful Coexistence, promote democracy in international relations through dialogue, communication, and cooperation. The internal affairs of a country should be decided by its people. International affairs should be discussed and solved by all countries on an equal footing. Developing countries ought to enjoy the equal right to participate in and make decisions on international affairs. All countries should respect each other and treat each other equally. No country is entitled to impose its own

will upon others, or maintain its security and development at the price of the interests of others. When handling international relations, it is necessary to proceed from the common interests of all the people throughout the world, make efforts to expand common interests, enhance understanding through communication, strengthen cooperation through understanding, and create a win-win situation through cooperation.

2. Upholding harmony and mutual trust to realize common security. All countries should join hands to respond to threats against world security. We should abandon the Cold War mentality, and cultivate a new security concept featuring mutual trust, mutual benefit, equality, and coordination. We should build a fair and effective collective security mechanism aimed at jointly preventing conflict and war, and cooperate to eliminate or reduce, as much as possible, threats from nontraditional security problems such as

Dove of Peace. This gilded dove of peace is a gift to the late Chinese leader, Deng Xiaoping, from UN Secretary-General Javier Perez de Guellar in May 1987.

terrorist activities, financial crises, and natural disasters, so as to safeguard world peace, security, and stability. We should persist in settling international disputes and conflicts peacefully through consultations and negotiations on the basis of equality, and work together to oppose acts of encroachment on the sovereignty of other countries, interference in the internal affairs of other countries, and willful use or threat of use of military force. We should step up a cooperative, resolute fight against terrorism, stamp out both the symptoms and root causes of terrorism, especially the root cause of the menace. We should achieve effective disarmament and arms control in a fair, rational, comprehensive, and balanced fashion, prevent the proliferation of weapons of mass destruction, vigorously promote the international nuclear disarmament process, and maintain global strategic stability.

3. **Upholding fairness and mutual benefit to achieve common development.** In the process of economic globalization, we should stick to the principle of fairness, achieve balanced and orderly development, and benefit all countries, developing countries in particular, instead of further widening the gap between North and South. We should propel economic globalization toward common prosperity. Developed countries should shoulder a greater responsibility for a universal, coordinated, and balanced development of the world, while developing countries should make full use of their own advantages to achieve development. We should actively further trade and investment liberalization, remove all kinds of trade barriers, increase market access, and ease restrictions on technology exports, so as to establish an international multilateral trading system that is public, fair, rational, transparent, open, and nondiscriminatory, and create a good trading environment conducive to orderly global economic development. We should further improve the international financial system to create a stable and highly efficient financial environment. We should step up worldwide dialogue and cooperation on energy, and jointly maintain energy security and energy market stability. We should actively promote and guarantee human rights to ensure that everyone enjoys equal opportunities and the right to pursue overall development. We should make innovations in development, promote the harmonious development of man and nature, and take the road of sustainable development.

4. **Upholding tolerance and creating an open society to achieve dialogue among civilizations.** Diversity of civilizations is a basic feature of human society, and an important driving force of human progress. All countries should respect other country's right to independently choose their own social systems and paths of development, learn from one another, and draw on the strong points of others to make up for their own weak points, thus achieving rejuvenation and development in line with their own national conditions. Dialogues and exchanges among civilizations should be

Chinese President Hu Jintao delivers a speech titled "Building a Harmonious World of Sustained Peace and Common Prosperity" at the summit meeting marking the 60th anniversary of the founding of the UN on September 15, 2005.

encouraged, and misgivings and estrangement between civilizations should be done away with. We should develop together by seeking common ground while putting aside differences, so as to make mankind more harmonious and the world more colorful. We should endeavor to preserve the diversity and development patterns of civilizations, and jointly build a harmonious world where all civilizations coexist with and accommodate one another.

The world today is facing unprecedented opportunities and challenges. However the situation changes, China is determined to hold high the banner of peace, development, and cooperation, persist in taking the road of peaceful development, pursue an opening-up strategy of mutual benefit with all as winners, and promote the building of a harmonious world based on enduring peace and common prosperity. This is a solemn commitment of the Chinese government!

THE NUMBER OF COUNTRIES WITH WHICH CHINA HAS ESTABLISHED DIPLOMATIC TIES

Period	No. of countries
1949–1959	32
1960–1969	17
1970–1979	67
1980–1989	16
1990–1999	34
Since 2000	5
Total	171

Chapter 2

Adhering to Independence, and Safeguarding Sovereignty and Security

Diplomacy is the official exercise of sovereignty externally by an independent state and an important means for a country to defend its interests and implement its foreign policy. Diplomatic independence is impossible without the independence of national sovereignty.

Ever since its founding, New China has achieved and consolidated its national and diplomatic independence, maintained national security and territorial integrity, and has gained equal status and dignity for China on the international stage. China cherishes its hard-won independence and respects the independence of other countries, and makes it the fundamental principle of its foreign policy.

The Development of Independent Foreign Policy

China's external relations and diplomacy in the 100 years before the founding of the PRC in 1949 were subjected to endless bullying and humiliation. After the first Opium War in 1940, the imperialist powers forced upon the late Qing government a series of unequal treaties by which they seized many prerogatives in China, including leaseholds, spheres of influence, open ports, extraterritorialities, and unilateral, most-favored nation status, among others. Countless Chinese people with noble ideals in recent history had waged tireless and arduous struggles for China's national independence and liberation, but all failed to change China's fate. By the time the People's Republic of China (PRC) was founded, the Western imperialists still enjoyed such privileges in China as stationing troops, carrying on free trade, inland river navigation, maintaining jurisdiction and customs administrations, and setting tariffs.

On October 1, 1949, the PRC was founded. Chinese people finally stood up. Thereafter, the main diplomatic task of New China has become safeguarding national independence, territorial integrity, and sovereignty.

It was imperative to do away with the prerogatives imperialists enjoyed in China, and have a clear break with the legacy of Old China's diplomacy of humiliation in order to achieve independence. The New Chinese government adopted and carried out three major foreign policies, namely "cleaning up the house before entertaining guests," "starting anew," and "leaning to one side."

To implement the policy of "cleaning up the house before entertaining guests," new laws were promulgated to gradually clear up the political, economic, and cultural prerogatives enjoyed by the imperialists. The implementation of this policy changed the situation that China had to depend upon other countries, making it an independent country in political, economic, and cultural realms.

The Soviet Union is the first country to establish diplomatic ties with New China on October 2, 1949.

To carry out the policy of "starting anew," it is imperative to cease the Old China's diplomacy of humiliation, and renounce the diplomatic relations the Old Chinese government had established with foreign countries, and start New China's diplomatic relations with foreign countries on the basis of equality. As for those who did not want to recognize or develop relations with the new Chinese government on an equal footing, China would not recognize the diplomatic missions accredited to old China as diplomatic envoys. As for the treaties or agreements made between the old Chinese government with foreign countries, the new Chinese government, after a review, would decide to recognize, abrogate, revise, or renegotiate according to their respective contents.

By pursuing the policy of "leaning to one side," New China took its stand in the socialist camps headed by the Soviet Union according to the different policies and attitudes of the United States and the Soviet Union toward New China in the context of the Cold War between the East and the West. Upon the founding of the PRC, the Common Program adopted by the Chinese People's Political Consultative Conference clearly states: "The People's Republic of China shall unite with all peace-loving and freedom-loving countries and peoples throughout the world, first of all, with the USSR, all peoples' democracies and all oppressed nations. It shall take its stand in the camp of international peace and democracy to oppose imperialist aggression, and to defend lasting world peace."

To carry out the policy of "leaning to one side," Chairman Mao Zedong paid a visit to the Soviet Union shortly after the founding of New China. The two sides signed in February 1950 the Sino-Soviet Treaty of Friendship, Alliance, and Mutual Assistance, in which the two parties undertook to cement Sino-Soviet friendly cooperation and jointly prevent a repetition of imperialist aggression. The Sino-Soviet treaty provided China with a reliable ally and a guarantee for its security.

Opposing the threats from superpowers and safeguarding national security was the main task for maintaining New China's independence in the early days after its founding. After the outbreak of the Korean War in June 1950, American President Harry Truman issued a declaration ordering US forces to intervene directly in the Korean War and the American seventh fleet to be deployed in the Taiwan Straits. He also increased the American military presence in the Philippines and the American military assistance to French troops in Indochina. Truman's declaration linked up the Korean Peninsula, Taiwan Straits, and Southeast Asia with the same target at the newly founded China. While intervening in the Korean War, US military aircraft intruded into China's airspace over Northeast China and bombed Chinese villages along the Sino-Korean border. At the same time, the US manipulated the UN, when the PRC's legitimate seat in the UN was deprived, and passed resolutions to impose sanctions against China. The US navy forced interrogations and examinations on

India's first Ambassador to China, K.M. Panikkar presents his credentials to Chairman Mao Zedong in May 1950.

Sweden is the first Western country to establish diplomatic relations with New China in June 1950.

Chinese commercial ships on the high seas, encroaching on the Chinese rights of free voyage and causing great damage and losses to Chinese people's lives and property.

China was forced to get involved in the Korean War, and in the end, won the war, and brought peace to the Korean Peninsula, meeting the goal of defending the country and protecting the people's home. This raised China's international status, and greatly enhanced its independence, sovereignty, and security. In Indochina, China supported the struggles of the Indochinese people for their national independence and actively participated in the Geneva conference, which restored peace to Indochina and eliminated the US threat from the south. Thereafter, the core and key issue in China's relations with the US shifted to the opposition of the US infringement upon the Chinese territory of Taiwan, and to the opposition of US interference in China's internal affairs. These have remained two of China's major foreign policy tasks until today.

Independence has been New China's fundamental diplomatic principle. It has been the defining feature that makes New China's diplomacy remarkably different from that of Old China and has penetrated every aspect of New China's diplomacy. During the 1950s when the "leaning to one side" policy was China's foreign policy strategy, Mao Zedong, Zhou Enlai, and other Chinese leaders repeatedly exhorted that China should not depend upon the Soviet Union too much or copy its experiences blindly. They said that China should think and act independently, and that "although strategically we are allies, tactically we should not relinquish our right of criticism." Due to the differences in their international positions, China and the Soviet Union began to differ on the international situation as well as diplomatic strategies, especially their strategies toward the US, from the late 1950s. The Soviet Union tried to bring China onto its track of "Soviet-US cooperation for world domination." Despite great pressure, Mao Zedong and other Chinese leaders declined the suggestion from USSR as it would undermine China's sovereignty and diplomatic independence, and upheld China's independence in developing its relations with other socialist countries.

The international situation underwent major changes in the late 1960s. The US was bogged down in the quagmire of the Vietnam War, while the Soviet Union seized the opportunity and started expansionism. After US President Richard Nixon took office, he put forward the Nixon Doctrine in an attempt to reduce the US presence in the Asia-Pacific region and the world as a whole. At the same time, the Soviet leader put forward the Brezhnev Doctrine, the core of which was that the Soviet Union was entitled to interfere in the internal affairs of other Socialist countries. The two doctrines symbolized the decrease of the US threat and the increase of the Soviet threat toward China. Realizing that the Soviet Union had become the major threat to China's security and world peace, China started to improve its relations with the US.

A group photo of the Chinese delegation to the Geneva Conference in 1954. The Delegation, headed by Chinese Premier and Foreign Minster Zhou Enlai, attended the conference aimed at seeking a peaceful solution to the Korean question and resumption of peace in Indochina from April to July 1954.

As the Soviet threat toward China increased, China started pursuing a policy strategy of opposing the two superpowers with a focus on opposing the Soviet hegemonism in the 1970s. In his meeting with foreign guests in 1973, Mao Zedong proposed: "The US, Japan, China, Pakistan, Iran, Turkey, the Arab World, and Europe, should be united; the Third-World countries must get united" to oppose the Soviet threat.

From the late 1970s to the early 1980s, the Soviet expansion encountered difficulties after its invasion of Afghanistan, while the US started to roll back the Soviets. The international balance of power witnessed a new shift to a virtue of balance between the two superpowers. The likelihood of war diminished and the threat China faced declined, making it possible for China to concentrate on domestic economic development. After the Third Plenary Session of the Eleventh CPC Central Committee in 1978, China placed more emphasis on the principle of independence in its foreign relations. In his opening remarks at the 12th National Congress of the CCP in 1982, Deng Xiaoping reiterated: "China's affairs should be run according to China's specific conditions and by the Chinese people themselves. Independence and self-reliance have always been, and will always be, their basic stand. While the Chinese people value their friendship and cooperation with other countries and peoples, they value even more their hard-won independence and sovereignty. No foreign country should expect China to be its vassal or to accept anything that is damaging to China's own interests."

A photo of China's first ambassador to France, Huang Zhen with French President De Gaulle. France was one of the first Western countries to establish diplomatic relations with China in January 1964.

After the Tiananmen Square Incident occurred in China in 1989, some Western countries, led by the US, made unwarranted charges against China, interfered in China's internal affairs, and even imposed sanctions on China. While meeting with foreign guests, Deng pointed out: "Sovereignty and national security should always be the priority." and "China will never allow any country to interfere in its internal affairs." The Chinese government carried on the peaceful foreign policy of independence, and successfully broke those sanctions.

Premier Zhou Enlai meets the US table tennis team in Beijing in April 1971. This visit opened the door to Sino-American contacts and was dubbed the Ping-pong diplomacy.

Having faced pressures from the West since the 1990s, China did not compromise or give in. Rather, it became more resolute in safeguarding its national sovereignty, national interests, and national dignity. In light of that, some countries advocated after the Cold War that "human rights are more important than sovereignty" and other theories that go against the purpose and principles of the UN Charter and infringe upon the principles of internal law and other international norms. China continued to adhere to the principle of independence, and was resolutely opposed to any country's interference in China's internal affairs for whatever reason.

The world has undergone tremendous changes since the end of the Cold War, and the traditional concept of security has evolved as well. In addition to territorial integrity and noninterference in sovereignty, which remain the major security issues, nontraditional security issues—such as economic security, cultural security, information security, ecological security, cross-border crimes, proliferation of nuclear technology, ethnic strife, drug trafficking, terrorism, and trans-border migrations— have become more and more salient. As the Report to the 17th National Congress the CCP states: "Whatever changes take place in the international arena, the Chinese government and people will always hold high the banner of peace, development, and cooperation, pursue an independent foreign policy of peace, safeguard China's interests in terms of sovereignty, security, and development, and uphold its foreign policy purposes of maintaining world peace and promoting common development."

The Contents of Independent Foreign Policy

Ever since its founding, the PRC's diplomatic strategies and foreign policies have undergone changes in response to the changing international situation; however, maintenance of independence has remained its basic theme. As a fundamental principle of Chinese foreign policy, independent foreign policy includes the following major aspects:

China is a unified, multinational country. Realizing national unity and maintaining national territorial integrity is a premise for independence and a notable manifestation of independent foreign policy. China can never tolerate an encroachment upon its national unity, territorial integrity, and national dignity. Under the complex domestic and international circumstances, opposing the threat to national unity and security from Taiwan independence, East Turkistan Islamic Movement, Tibet Independence, and other secessionist forces is one premise and fundamental task for China's independent foreign policy.

Sovereignty is the fundamental attribute and symbol of nation states. China holds that sovereign countries have the right to choose for themselves their own social system, independently determine their domestic and foreign policy, and choose their own road of national development without external inference. On international affairs, China values the rights of every people to choose their own roads of development by themselves, does not interfere in the international affairs of other countries, and does not impose its will on others, nor does China permit any other countries to interfere in China's internal affairs.

By upholding independence, China advocates the democratization of international affairs. Countries, big or small, strong or weak, rich or poor, are all equal members of the international community. They should enjoy the same and equal rights and shoulder the same and equal obligation on issues that concern world peace and the development of human beings as a whole. On international affairs, China holds that all countries should uphold the purposes and principles of the United Nations Charter, and observe international law and other universally recognized norms of international relations. Politically, all countries should respect each other and conduct consultations on an equal footing. Economically, they should cooperate with each other, draw on

Head of Chinese delegation Deng Xiaoping delivers a speech on China's principles on foreign relations at the 6th Special Session of the UN General Assembly in April 1974.

each other's strengths, and work together to advance economic globalization in the direction of balanced development, shared benefits, and win-win progress. Culturally, they should learn from each other in the spirit of seeking common ground while shelving differences, respecting the diversity of the world, and making joint efforts to advance human civilization. On environmental issues, they should assist and cooperate with each other to take good care of the Earth.

By holding independence, China supports any activities that are conducive to maintaining world strategic balance and stability. China holds that countries should enhance mutual understanding and trust, and endeavor to solve international disputes and conflicts through peaceful means. China advocates the new concept of security of mutual trust and mutual benefit, and equality and cooperation, to maintain regional and global security through cooperation of mutual benefits. China advocates solving international disputes through consultation and proposes seeking stability through cooperation and meeting the common challenges facing the world through enhancing multilateral security cooperation. China opposes the use or threat of use of force, and also opposes the policies of war, aggression, expansion, and the arms race.

In upholding independence, China does not enter into any alliances with any big powers or power blocks, or form military blocks, or engage in the arms race or military expansion. China pursues a national defense policy that is defensive in nature. It does not seek spheres of influence; neither does it support one country opposing another. China opposes hegemonism and commits that it will never seek hegemony, engage in expansionism, or pose a military threat to any other country.

In upholding independence, China develops friendly cooperation of mutual benefit with all countries according to the five principles of peaceful coexistence. China does not decide its relations with other countries according to any ideological standards or social systems. China is "prepared to maintain contacts and make friends with everyone."

China is not influenced or controlled by any specific issue at any specific time. Rather it is determined to develop omnidirectional relations with all countries with a view to maintaining world peace and promoting economic development.

In upholding independence, China never yields to any external pressure. Rather it decides its position and policy on international issues by considering the interests of the people of China and the world at large, the merits of

The 17th National Congress of the Chinese Communist Party in session in Beijing in October 2007. The political report delivered at this congress states that China will adhere to the independent foreign policy of peace.

the issues themselves, whether it is conducive to maintaining world peace and stability, whether it can promote cooperation among countries, and contribute to the prosperity of the world economy, culture, and human progress.

Safeguarding National Unity and Territorial Integrity

One premise for diplomatic independence is to realize and maintain national unity and secure national territorial integrity. China's foreign policy of independence is first reflected in its consistent opposition to foreign interference in China's internal affairs, in its struggle for reunification of the two sides of the Taiwan Straits, and in its diplomatic practice to resume the exercise of sovereignty over Hong Kong and Macau.

Taiwan is an inalienable part of the Chinese territory. After the war against China in 1895, Japan forced the Qing Government to sign the Treaty of Shimonoseki, and occupied Taiwan thereafter. In December 1943, the governments of China, the US, and Great Britain issued the Cairo Declaration, which stipulated that Japan return all the territories that it had seized or occupied, including Northeast China, Taiwan, and Penghu to China. The Potsdam Proclamation signed by China, the US, and Great Britain on July 26, 1945, which was subsequently adhered to by the Soviet Union, reiterated that the terms of the Cairo Declaration shall be carried out. In August of the same year, Japan surrendered. The condition of the surrender was that Japan accepted the provisions in the declaration. On October 25, the Chinese government recovered Taiwan and Penghu, and resumed sovereignty over Taiwan. Taiwan and Penghu had been put back under the jurisdiction of Chinese sovereignty not only de jure but de facto.

The government of the PRC was founded on October 1, 1949, replacing the government of the Republic of China (ROC) to become the sole legitimate government of all China and the only legitimate representative of China internationally. Some of the ruling Nationalist Party and the administrative officials of the old ROC government withdrew to Taiwan, creating a situation of separation on the two sides of the Taiwan Straits.

Against the backdrop of East-West confrontation, the US deployed its seventh fleet to the Taiwan Straits when the Korean War broke out in 1950, and signed a Mutual Defense Treaty with the Taiwan authorities in 1954, bringing China's Taiwan Province under US "protection." The US policy infringed upon China's territorial integrity and sovereignty, causing long-lasting tension along the Taiwan Straits.

The Taiwan question is a result of the Chinese civil war. Seeking reunification between Taiwan and the Chinese mainland is purely a Chinese domestic affair. The Chinese government has consistently opposed any interference by any country in China's internal affairs on the Taiwan question.

The US has been the most important foreign country supporting Taiwan's confrontation with the mainland, and prevents China from reaching national reunification. In the Joint Communiqué issued in Shanghai during Nixon's visit to China in 1972, the US stated: "The United States acknowledges that all Chinese on either side of the Taiwan Straits maintain that there is but one China and Taiwan is part of China. The United States does not challenge this position."

In December 1978, the US government accepted the three preconditions raised by the Chinese government for establishing diplomatic relations—that the US sever its diplomatic ties with Taiwan, abrogate the Mutual Defense Treaty signed by the US and the Taiwan authority, and withdraw its troops from Taiwan. After that, China and the US issued another joint communiqué on establishing diplomatic ties between the two countries. The communiqué provides: "The United States of America recognizes the Government of the People's Republic of China as the sole legal government of China. Within this context, the people of the United States will maintain cultural, commercial, and other unofficial relations with the people of Taiwan. . .The government of the United States of America acknowledges the Chinese position that there is but one China and Taiwan is part of China."

Taiwan compatriots on the Great Wall. In October 1987, the Taiwan authorities began to allow compatriots in Taiwan to visit their relatives on the mainland.

China hoped that the relaxation of bilateral relations and the final establishment of diplomatic ties between China and the US would facilitate the reunification of the two sides of the Taiwan Straits. When Sino-US diplomatic ties were established, the Chinese government, in order to promote world peace, made a change to the policy of "we must liberate Taiwan"—a policy China had promoted ever since its founding—and proposed the "one country, two systems" formula in an attempt to realize a peaceful reunification of the motherland.

However, the US abandoned its policy of not interfering in China's internal affairs on the Taiwan issue after China and the US established diplomatic ties. In March 1979, the US Congress passed a so-called Taiwan Relations Act, which contains many provisions that contradict the Sino-US joint communiqué and the principles of international law, including provisions that the US will continue to sell weapons to Taiwan.

The US sales of weapons to Taiwan caused the first crisis in Sino-US relations after their normalizations. In order to solve the problems of American arms sales to Taiwan, the Chinese government and the US government reached another agreement in August 1982 through negotiation, and the two sides issued the third joint communiqué on bilateral relations. The US government states in the communiqué: "It (the US government) does not seek to carry out a long-term policy of arms sales to Taiwan, that its arms sales to Taiwan will not exceed, either in qualitative or in quantitative terms, the level of those supplied in recent years since the establishment of diplomatic relations between the United States and China, and that it intends gradually to reduce its sale of arms to Taiwan, leading, over a period of time, to a final resolution."

As Sino-US relations stabilized in the 1980s, the cross-straits relations also relaxed. Nonofficial exchanges between the two sides of the Taiwan Straits started in 1987. After the end of the Cold War, the Taiwan authorities changed its policy on reunification and gradually deviated from the one-China stand to seek Taiwan independence in the name of so-called "expanding (Taiwan's) international space." The Taiwan authorities had made attempts to participate in the United Nations since 1993, and Lee Teng-hui, the leader of Taiwan regime, even referred to the cross-straits relations as "special state-to-state relations.". During this process, the US government has time and again broken its commitments made in the August 17 Joint Communiqué, and upgraded its arms sales to Taiwan both in quantitative and qualitative terms. The US decision to sell Taiwan 150 F-16s fighter planes in 1992, and the package of advanced weapons sold to Taiwan in 2001 and 2008 all violated its commitments on this issue, creating obstacles and new external blocks for the peaceful settlement of the Taiwan question. Such American moves have been strongly opposed by the Chinese government and have resulted in several frictions and crises in bilateral relations.

China not only opposes the US sale of weapons to Taiwan, but also opposes any other countries selling weapons to Taiwan or entering into a military alliance with the Taiwan authorities. The Netherlands government, disregarding the Chinese government's opposition, insisted on selling weapons to Taiwan, which led to a downgrade of the bilateral relations in 1982. The French government's decision to sell weapons to Taiwan in 1992 also caused big twists and turns in Sino-French relations, which did not return to normal until after the French government reaffirmed its policy on this issue.

As the sole legitimate government of China in the world, the PRC has a clear and consistent policy on Taiwan. There is but one China and Taiwan is an inalienable part of Chinese territory, and all countries that have diplomatic ties with China should respect her sovereignty and territorial integrity. China strongly opposes any country that has diplomatic relations with China such as treating Taiwan as an "independent political entity," or establishing or developing official ties with Taiwan, or creating "dual recognition" in whatever form, or creating "two Chinas" or "one China, one Taiwan." This is a principle the PRC has insisted upon in developing its relations with other countries.

The Chinese government safeguards all the legitimate rights and interests of Taiwan compatriots abroad. On the basis of the one-China principle, the Chinese government has made arrangements for Taiwan's participation in

Wang Daohan, Chairman of the Association for Relations across the Taiwan Straits from the mainland, and Koo Chen-fu, Chairman of the Straits Exchange Foundation from Taiwan, hold talks in Singapore in April 1993. This was the first meeting of the top leaders of authorized nongovernmental organizations from both sides of the Taiwan Straits.

The 5th Cross-Straits Economic, Trade, and Culture Forum is held in Changsha, Hunan Province in July 2009.

some intergovernmental international organizations that accept regional memberships in an agreeable and acceptable way according to the nature, regulations, and actual conditions of these international organizations. As a region of China, Taiwan has participated in the Asian Development Bank (ADB) and the Asia-Pacific Economic Cooperation (APEC) in the name of Chinese Taipei, and the World Trade Organization as a separate Taiwan-Penghu-Jinmen-Mazu tariff zone.

However the situation changes, the Chinese government is committed to the policy of "one country, two systems" and peaceful reunification, and will make its utmost effort with an utmost sincerity to promote the peaceful development of cross-straits relations in an attempt to realize peaceful reunification. But it has also made clear that it will never allow anyone to split Taiwan from the motherland in any form or in whatever name. The Anti-Secession Law passed by the Chinese National People's Congress in 2005 reaffirmed in legal terms the Chinese government's policy of peaceful reunification of the two sides of the Taiwan Straits, but it also provides that "if the Taiwan secessionist forces should act under any name or by any means to cause the fact of Taiwan's secession from China, or that major incidents entailing Taiwan's secession from China should occur, or that possibilities for a peaceful reunification should be completely exhausted, the state shall employ nonpeaceful means and other necessary measures to protect China's sovereignty and territorial integrity."

Resuming the Exercise of Sovereignty over Hong Kong and Macau in Accordance with the Principle of "One Country, Two Systems"

The "one country, two systems" formula was initially put forward for the settlement of the Taiwan question, but was first successfully implemented in China's resuming the exercise of sovereignty over Hong Kong and Macau.

Hong Kong has been part of Chinese territory since the British army invaded and occupied Hong Kong Island during the first Opium War in 1840. According to the Treaty of Nanking imposed onto the Qing government by the British in 1842, Hong Kong was ceded to Britain. In 1856, the British and French launched the Second Opium War and compelled the Qing government to conclude the Convention of Peking in 1860, which led to the cession from China of the southern region of the Kowloon Peninsula. In the wake of the Sino-Japanese War (1894–1895), Britain forced the Qing government to sign the Convention for the Extension of Hong Kong Territory in 1898, according to which the new territories and 262 neighboring islands were leased to Britain for 99 years, a contract which expired on June 30, 1997. The ceding of Hong Kong to Britain was one of the most humiliating episodes in Chinese history.

In conformity with the changing international situation, Deng Xiaoping put forward the idea of "one country, two systems" to solve the problem of national reunification after 1978. "One country, two systems" means that, under the one-China premise, the main part of the country keeps its socialist system, while Hong Kong and Macau, as an inalienable part of China, retain their capitalist system and way of life for a long period of time to come as special administrative regions.

In accordance with the above policy, the Chinese government and the government of Britain signed, after rounds of negotiation, the Joint Declaration in December 1984, which provided the time, policies, and arrangements during the transition for the return of Hong Kong, laying out rules that could be followed for the final settlement of the Hong Kong issue.

In 1985, the Chinese National People's Congress established a Basic Law Drafting Committee for the Hong Kong Special Administrative Region of China. The Basic Law for the Hong Kong Special Administrative Region, passed in April 1990, specifies in clear and concrete terms the relations between the Central Government and the Hong Kong Special Administrative Region, the basic rights and obligations of the people in Hong Kong, the political and economic system as well as the foreign affairs in Hong Kong. This had paved the way for China to resume sovereignty over Hong Kong.

Chairman Mao Zedong meets with visiting British ex-Prime Minister Edward Heath in May 1974. The hosts and guests discussed the Hong Kong question.

In the early days after the signing of the Sino-British Joint Declaration in 1984, the two sides cooperated well and smoothly. However, the British Hong Kong authorities misjudged the situation after the end of the Cold War, went against the spirit of the Joint Declaration and other relevant agreements reached between China and Britain on Hong Kong's return, and prepared to have a "democratic" reform in Hong Kong during the transition or before the PRC resumed sovereignty. The British intended to establish a "democratic" system in Hong Kong during the last years of British rule so as to retain its political and economic influence in Hong Kong after it was returned to China.

Such policies of the British Hong Kong authorities were rejected resolutely by the Chinese government. At midnight of June 30, 1997 a grand ceremony of Hong Kong's return to China was held at Hong Kong Conference and Exhibition Hall. At the same time, the Chinese troops took over Hong Kong's defense duty, starting the exercise of sovereignty over Hong Kong.

The problem of Macau has similarities with the Hong Kong situation. The Portuguese landed in Macau to engage in trade in 1535 and started to live there in 1557. Portugal forced the Qing government to sign the Sino-Portuguese Protocol of Lisbon and Sino-Portuguese Treaty of Beijing in March and December of 1887, respectively. From then on the Portuguese had occupied and lived in Macau and treated it as a Portuguese territory.

The heads of government of China and Britain formally sign the Sino-British Joint Declaration on the Hong Kong Question in Beijing on December 19, 1984.

After its formation in 1949, the PRC government stated on many occasions that Macau has always been Chinese territory and that the question of Macau was a question left over from the past. The Chinese government held that the questions should be settled through negotiations when conditions were ripe, and that, pending a settlement, the status quo should be maintained for the time being.

The settlement of the Hong Kong question provided a model for settling the question of Macau. The Chinese government and the Portuguese government signed a Joint Declaration on Macau in April 1987, which stipulated that the PRC would resume sovereignty over Macau on December 20, 1999.

The Basic Law for the Macau Special Administrative Region was passed in March 1993 by the Chinese National People's Congress. On December 19, 1999 the Chinese government and the Portuguese government jointly held a solemn ceremony for the return of Macau to the motherland.

The return of Hong Kong and Macau to China made the people in Hong Kong and Macau the true owner of these two regions, put an end to Western colonialism in China, and ushered in a new era for Hong Kong and Macau.

Ever since their return, Hong Kong and Macau have achieved social stability and economic prosperity under the efficient leadership of the two special administrative regions and the strong support from the Chinese central

China and Britain hold a ceremony for the return of Hong Kong on July 1, 1999.

Leaders of China and Portugal toast the Sino-Portuguese Joint Statement on the Macau Questions, formally signed in Beijing on April 13, 1987.

government. The successful practice of "one country, two systems" in Hong Kong and Macau has paved the way for the final settlement of the Taiwan question and the eventual reunification for China.

Opposing National Separation, and Safeguarding National Unity

China is a unified, multiethnic country, with 56 ethnic groups. All these ethnic groups witnessed fusion during their formation and evolution. During this long historical process, frequent migration of each group resulted in the distribution pattern of China's ethnic groups living together over vast areas while some live in individual concentrated communities in small areas. The Han Chinese people have the largest population, scattered all over the country. In spite of small populations mainly inhabiting remote areas, ethnic minorities can also be seen living in the county-level or higher level administrative regions in the hinterland of China. This fact determines that it is conducive to maintaining a harmonious and stable interethnic relationship and seeking common development to establish autonomous local governments of ethnic minorities in various types and levels on the basis of concentrated areas of ethnic minorities. This system of regional ethnic autonomy was provided for in the Constitution of People's Republic of China adopted by the 1st National People's Congress in 1954, and remains in the constitution after several amendments.

Given the sophisticated situation of today, China's diplomacy faces the task of safeguarding national unity and opposing national separation, and the Tibet and Xinjiang issues are especially salient.

Tibet is an inseparable part of China and Tibetans are an important member of the multiethnic Chinese family. The Tibetans have lived on the Tibetan plateau for generations and created a magnificent culture, which is a precious property of the Chinese culture.

Tibet in history was under the despotic feudal serf system marked by a combination of government and religion that was worse than the system in Europe during the Middle Ages. Although the slave owners accounted for less than five percent of the Tibetan population, they owned all the means of production and educational resources. The Dalai Lama, the head of the Tibetan Buddhism and Tibetan local government, controlled all the religious and administrative power.

Tibet was liberated through peaceful negotiation in 1951. In 1959, a democratic reform was carried out in Tibet, and the despotic feudal serf system was abolished. The 14th Dalai Lama went in exile abroad. Over the past half a century, the Chinese government has placed great emphasis on the protection and development of Tibetan culture according to the Constitution of the People's Republic of China and the Law of Regional National Autonomy. Meanwhile, the Chinese government has also tried its best to develop modern science and upgrade the educational system there.

The Dalai clique, turning a blind eye to the truth and taking religion as its cover, spread the rumor of "the extinction of traditional Tibetan culture" in the world, demanding a withdrawal of the Chinese army and its military facilities from Tibet in an attempt to realize the so-called "Independence of the Great Tibetan Zone." In order to draw the attention of the international community, the Dalai clique has also instigated riots and created social instability, causing injuries, deaths, and losses in Tibet.

The Chinese government is firmly against any activity aimed to separate the country and have Tibetans seek independence. China holds that the Dalai Lama issue is by no means a religious issue, but a political one. The 14th Dalai Lama is more a political refugee engaging in splitting the motherland, rather than a religious figure. China is of the view that as long as the Dalai Lama genuinely gives up his divisive stand, stops his activities to split the motherland, admits in public that Tibet is an inalienable part of China, and that the government of the PRC is the sole legitimate government representing the whole of China, the central government is willing to contact and negotiate with him on his personal arrangement in the future.

The fact that Tibet is an inalienable part of China has been recognized by all the governments around the world. There is not a single government that has recognized Tibet's "independence" or the so-called "Tibetan government in exile." The so-called Tibet problem was, in the first place, the result of imperialists vainly attempting to carve up China, and to turn China into their colony or semicolony. After the Dalai clique defected abroad, some anti-China forces have continued to support "Tibetan independence" activities of the Dalai clique. Therefore, the so-called Tibet problem is by no means an ethnic minority issue, a religious issue, or a human rights issue, but an issue concerning the Western anti-China forces' conspiracy of containing, splitting, and demonizing China. China is firmly against the Dalai Lama visiting any foreign country to promote activities of splitting China in any capacity, and against any country providing facilities and forums that support the Dalai Lama's activities of splitting China.

Xinjiang is also an inalienable part of Chinese territory. Xinjiang Uygur Autonomous Region was founded in 1955. For half a century, Xinjiang has made great progress in all aspects of economy and society. After the end of the Cold War, under the influence of religious extremism, ethnic separatism, and international terrorism, East Turkistan Islamic Movement forces both inside and outside China have resorted to separating and sabotaging activities with terrorist violence as their chief means. They have plotted a number of incidents of terror and violence, seriously jeopardizing the lives, property, and security of the Chinese people of various ethnic groups, and posing a threat to the security and stability of the countries and regions concerned.

After the September 11 Incident, the calling for international cooperation on the war against terrorism became very strong. In order to get out of their predicament, the East Turkistan forces once again raised the banner of "human rights," "freedom of religion," and "interests of ethnic minorities," and have fabricated claims that "the Chinese government is using every opportunity to oppress ethnic minorities." This is done to mislead the public and deceive world opinion in order to escape blows dealt by the international struggle against terrorism. At the same time, they have constantly conspired for various terrorist incidents jeopardizing regional peace and stability, and thus have become the target of the Shanghai Five and Shanghai Cooperation Organization.

In September 2002, the UN Security Council included the East Turkistan Islamic Movement on its list of terrorist organizations. China has always actively participated in international cooperation against terrorism. China opposes any double standard on anti-terrorism and any support by any country in any pretext to any terrorist and separatist activities intending to split the country.

Chapter 3

Participating in Multilateral Diplomacy, and Playing a Constructive Role

The relationship between modern China and the world has witnessed such a historic change that China's future has been closely bound up with that of the world. China is promoting the world's development and prosperity through its own development and prosperity, and playing a constructive and responsible role in maintaining world peace and advancing human progress. China's active participation in multilateral diplomacy, its constructive role in international affairs, and its efforts to push for a more just and rational international order have become the most active aspects of China's foreign relations.

Participating in International Institutions, and Promoting Multilateral Diplomacy

Throughout world history, conflicts and wars occurred among ancient civilizations, leading to their rise, fall, and fusion. The Chinese civilization is remarkable in that it has, in general, managed to maintain its main characteristics and integrity despite its contact with others in history. This is due to the fact that the Chinese civilization was separated from the Indian civilization in the Southwest by the Himalayas, and from those in the Middle East and Europe by vast deserts and plateaus in the Northwest. The Chinese civilization is the only one of the four great civilizations that has survived and continues until today.

The presidents of China, Russia, Kazakhstan, Kyrgyzstan, Tajikistan, and Uzbekistan meet for the first time and sign the Declaration on the Establishment of the Shanghai Cooperation Organization in June 2001.

In recent history, the West became strong economically after it took the lead in industrialization, and promoted global economic integration and cultural collisions and fusions. China's door was forced open by Western countries with warships and cannons, reducing China to a semicolonial and semifeudal country from a "Celestial Empire." During this bloody process of humiliation, a fair number of people with lofty ideals made various attempts to rescue China. The Westernization Movement characterized by "Chinese learning for essence and Western for practical use" failed after the Sino-Japanese war (1894–1895). The reform movement of 1898 lasted only for 100 days. The Revolution of 1911 succeeded in overthrowing the feudal ruling, but still failed to uplift China's international status. China was in the end drawn into the international system passively and plunged into a subordinate position.

Led by the Communist Party of China, the Chinese people of all ethnic groups overthrew the rule of imperialism, feudalism, and bureaucratic capitalism, won the new democratic revolution, and founded the People's Republic of China in 1949 after hard, protracted, and tortuous struggles. New China's government hoped that China could establish relations with Western countries based on the principle of equality and mutual respect, and that China could participate in the international community and render its contribution to world peace and prosperity.

APEC leaders pose for a group photo in Shanghai, China. In October 2001 the annual Informal Meeting of Asia-Pacific Economic Cooperation Leaders was held in Shanghai.

Soon after the founding of New China, Premier and Foreign Minister Zhou Enlai sent a telegraph to then UN Secretary General Lie, demanding that the UN expel the representatives of the Taiwan authorities, and informed the UN that New China had appointed Zhang Wentian as the permanent representative of China to the UN. Due to US obstruction, China's demand was not accepted. After the Korean War, the United States manipulated the United Nations to shelve the discussion of China's legitimate seat in the UN under the pretext of the Korean War. Constrained by the division of international political forces and Cold War confrontation, China's contacts with the international community were initially limited to its relations with the Soviet Union, East European socialist countries, and a few neighboring countries.

After the Sino-Soviet relations deteriorated in the 1960s, China was not only in confrontation with Western countries in the international system, but its relations with socialist countries were terribly affected. In the wake of the Cultural Revolution, China was once again trapped in isolation as it withdrew from the few international organizations that it had only just joined, and even ceased to participate in some international sports contests for a while.

The 1970s witnessed positive changes in China's relationship with the international community. On October 26, 1971, the United Nations General Assembly adopted, at its 26th session, Resolution 1758, which expelled the representatives of the Taiwan authorities and restored the seat and all the lawful

Jubilant Chinese delegates at the 26th UN General Assembly. The legitimate seat of the PRC was restored in October 1971.

rights of the government of the PRC in the United Nations, which marked an important step of China's participation in international organizations and integration into the international system. By 1977, China had joined 21 international organizations including the UN, and had signed off on 45 international treaties, agreements, and conventions.

The year of 1978 was a turning point in Chinese history. China began to practice an opening-up policy, which was carried out gradually from the coastal areas to the interior of China. While working hard to "invite foreign organizations and investors in," China took an active step to "go out" by actively participating in the activities of the UN, starting the process of integration into the international system. In the realm of the economy, China joined the World Bank and the International Monetary Fund (IMF) in 1980, and resumed its observer status in the General Agreement and Tariff and Trade (GATT) in 1982. China formally applied for the restoration of its contracting party status in GATT in 1986. In the realm of security, China began, in 1980, to participate in the Conference on Disarmament in Geneva and its affiliated special committees and working groups. By the end of 1986, China had joined the UN and all of its affiliated multilateral organizations.

A group photo of Chinese President Hu Jintao with leaders of other countries at the North-South Informal Summit in Evian, France, in June 2003.

The Forum of China-African Cooperation Beijing Summit is held in Beijing in November 2006.

The end of the Cold War removed the political obstacles of exchanges between the East and the West, and the world economy was integrated into a whole. Globalization has blurred the border between domestic and international issues, and many problems facing human kind, such as environmental problems, epidemic diseases, energy deficiency, migrant problems, and trans-boundary crimes are becoming convergent, and they cannot be solved by a single country. In security areas, the end of the Cold War erased the possibility of large-scale wars between superpowers. On the one hand, the international situation relaxed in general; on the other, various traditional security problems are still far from being solved while nontraditional security problems become prominent. Multilateral cooperation on international security issues becomes an important field of multilateral diplomacy in the post-Cold War era.

Demand for the international community to reinforce coordination and broaden cooperation to address common challenges has been on the rise. International organizations are becoming more important, and multilateral diplomacy has become more active than ever before.

In the context of globalization in the post-Cold War era, China has unswervingly followed the policy of opening up, adapted itself to the trend

Chinese Primer Wen Jiabao attends the opening ceremony of the 6th Asia-European Summit in Finland in September 2006.

Margaret Chan Fung Fu-chun, former Director of Health of China's Hong Kong Special Administrative Region Government, is elected the Director-General of the World Health Organization in November 2006. She is the first elected head to a special organization of the UN nominated by China.

of economic globalization, and actively participated in international economic cooperation and competition. While making full use of the beneficial conditions and opportunities of economic globalization, China is fully aware of the risks that result from economic globalization. China has joined more international regimes and expanded its multilateral diplomacy, making it more integrated into the international community.

By 2008 China had joined more than 130 intergovernmental organizations and thousands of nongovernmental international organizations, including such international organizations as the UN, G8+5 and G20, regional international organizations such as the Shanghai Cooperation Organization and ASEAN+3 Dialogue Mechanism, and transregional international organizations such as the Asian-European Summit, APEC and China-Africa Cooperation Forum. China had also signed or acceded to 300 multilateral international treaties, conventions, agreements, and protocols compared to 157 in 1989, covering the fields of politics, security, economy, culture, and so on.

While integrating into the international community, China has followed an open win-win strategy of mutual benefit. This strategy calls for China

Leaders present at the 2008 annual meeting of the Bo'ao Forum for Asia pose for photo. The forum has been held annually in Hainan, China since 2002.

to promote regional and global development by its own development, and extend the convergence of interests with other parties. In participating in international organizations, China has maintained multilateralism and open regionalism. As a developing country, China has actively engaged in summit diplomacy, advocated China's views, expanded its relations with other countries, and taken due responsibilities and obligations while safeguarding China's interests and improving its global image. China has played a constructive role in solving global and regional problems. For instance, China spearheaded the Bo'ao Forum, promoted the establishment of the Shanghai Cooperation Organization, and hosted the six-party talks on the Korean nuclear issue. China has gradually changed its mode of passive participation in multilateral organizations, becoming an active participator, an advocator, and a leader in multilateral diplomacy.

The relationship between modern China and the world has undergone historic changes. China's economy has become a vital part of the world economy, and China has become an important member of the international system. China's future has been closely bound up with that of the world. China cannot realize its development while being isolated from the world, nor can the world have its prosperity and stability without China. China is promoting global development and prosperity with its own development and prosperity.

Playing a Constructive Role in the United Nations

The United Nations is the most universal, representative, and authoritative intergovernmental organization in the world and its membership has grown from 51 at its founding to today's 192. The UN activities and functions now cover politics, economy, security, human rights, and other social affairs in the post-Cold War era.

As one of the founding members of the UN and one of the permanent members of the UN Security Council, China has placed great emphasis on the role of the UN, participated actively in the UN's work in all aspects and all fields, and rendered its full support to the UN.

After China had its legitimate seat in the UN restored, it sent high-ranking delegates to the annual general assembly meeting, elaborating China's stances and views on global and regional issues. Given the enhanced role of the UN in international affairs after the Cold War, Chinese leaders have attended all the important meetings within the UN framework.

Chinese President Jiang Zemin attended the United Nations Millennium Summit in 2000 and elaborated to the world the Chinese government's support

Leaders of the five permanent members of the UN Security Council meet during the Millennium Summit of the United Nations in September 2000 at China's suggestion.

of the organization. He stated that the active role of the UN must be strengthened, not weakened, and its authority defended, not jeopardized, in the new situation. China has firmly defended the purposes and principles of the UN Charter and held that the UN and its Security Council should continue to play an active role in handling international affairs and safeguarding world peace, and ensure that all its member states enjoy equal rights in participating in world affairs.

President Hu Jintao was present at the Conference in Commemoration of the 60th anniversary of the founding of the UN in 2005. He proposed at the conference that the UN and other multilateral mechanisms should continue to play their constructive role in solving international disputes, maintaining peace, providing humanitarian aid, and many other fields. He also elaborated on China's diplomatic thought of "building a harmonious world of sustained peace and common prosperity."

While supporting the UN's important role, China has played an increasingly important, positive, and constructive role in maintaining world peace and settling international and regional hotspot issues under

High Level International Conference on Millennium Development Goals is held in Beijing in March 2004.

the framework of the UN. Examples include China's participation in the UN peacekeeping operations, promotion of arms control and disarmament, and cooperation in human rights affairs within the framework of the UN, among others.

Participation in the UN Peace Keeping Operations

Peacekeeping operations are one of the important means for the UN to perform its duty in maintaining international peace and security as stipulated by the UN Charter. Since the 36th general assembly of the UN in 1981, China has adopted a positive attitude toward the role of UN peacekeeping operations in relaxing tensions. China began to pay its due to UN peacekeeping operations in 1982 and became a member of the UN Special Committee on Peacekeeping Operations in 1988. By June 2008, China had sent more than 10,000 military personnel and police to 24 UN peacekeeping operations, during which three Chinese officers and five soldiers laid down their precious lives for the missions.

The second group of peacekeeping troops of the Chinese PLA leaves China for its mission in Cambodia in February 1993.

CHRONICLE OF CHINA'S PARTICIPATION IN UN PEACEKEEPING

- In January 1982, China began to pay its due to the UN peacekeeping operations.
- In April 1989, China joined the special committee on Peacekeeping Operations.
- In November 1989, China sent nonmilitary personnel to the UN peacekeeping operations for the first time.
- In April 1990, China sent military observers to the UN peacekeeping operations for the first time.
- In April 1992, China sent noncombat units to serve in UN peacekeeping operations.
- In January 2000, China first sent civilian police to UN peacekeeping operations.
- In January 2002, China formally participated in the Class-A stand-by arrangements mechanism for the UN peacekeeping operations. Class-A mechanism stipulates that personnel and equipments are to be deployed in position within 90 days.

In September 2007, the Chinese major general Zhao Jingmin was designated as commander in chief for the United Nations mission for referendum in Western Sahara, and became the first Chinese serviceman serving as a senior commander of the UN peacekeeping forces.

China holds that the UN shall play an irreplaceable role in peacekeeping, which should comply with the purposes and principles of the UN Charter and other universally recognized norms of international relations, especially the principles of respecting the sovereignty of all countries and noninterference in other countries' internal affairs, obtaining agreement from the country concerned beforehand, maintaining neutrality and nonuse of force except for self-defense. China believes that these principles are essential to the smooth and successful implementation of the peacekeeping missions.

Promoting Disarmament within the United Nations Framework

China is one of the five permanent members of the UN Security Council and a nuclear power. Since the very day China had nuclear weapons, it has solemnly undertaken not to use or threaten to use nuclear weapons against nonnuclear-weapon states or nuclear-weapon-free zones. Since China formally joined in the work of the Geneva Conference on Disarmament and its sub-committees and working groups in 1980, it has actively attended the annual meetings of the First Committee of the United Nations General Assembly that deliberates issues on disarmament and international security. China has been present at the annual conference of the Disarmament Commission of the UN. China has supported the United Nations' important role in nonproliferation. It has so far acceded to all the international treaties on nonproliferation, joined in the relevant international organizations, and has so far established a comprehensive legal system for export control of nuclear, biological, chemical, missile, and related dual-use items and technologies.

In the realm of conventional weapons control, China has earnestly fulfilled its obligations under the Convention on Certain Conventional Weapons (CCW) and its additional protocols. It has taken concrete measures to ensure that its anti-personnel landmines in service meet the relevant technical requirements of the Amended Protocol on Landmines. China actively participates in the work of the Group of Governmental Experts (GGE) on Cluster Munitions, and is preparing to ratify the Protocol on Explosive Remnants of War.

Qian Qichen, Vice Premier and Foreign Minister of China, signs the Comprehensive Test Ban Treaty (CTBT) at the United Nations Headquarters in New York in September 1996.

The China Arms Control and Disarmament Association is set up on August 21, 2001. The association was the first nongovernmental organization for arms control in China.

In addition, China has taken strides to reduce its military personnel and increase its military transparency. The Central Military Committee of the Chinese government decided to cut its military personnel by one million in 1985 and it went another step forward in 1997 by resolving to cut another half a million in three years. A third cut was made in 2003 by another 200,000 in two years, bringing China's total military force to 2.3 million.

Promoting Human Rights within the Framework of the UN and International Cooperation on Human Rights Issues

One of the principal aims of the United Nations is to promote and encourage the respect for human rights and fundamental freedoms of human beings, and protecting and promoting human rights are the goals of the United Nations Charter.

China began to participate in the United Nations human rights conference as an observer in 1979, and was elected to the Human Rights Commission in the Economic and Social Council of the United Nations in 1981. China has been on the Human Rights Commission since 1982 and has attended in the annual meetings ever since.

After the end of the Cold War, some countries made use of the human rights issue to criticize and interfere in other countries' internal affairs, making human rights one of the focal contradictions between the North and the South.

Chinese President Hu Jintao meets with the UN Secretary General Kofi Annan in Beijing in October 2004.

China sets store by human rights and has promulgated or revised many of its laws to protect and promote human rights. China is not against the discussion of human rights with other countries on the basis of equality and mutual respect, but China opposes interference in its internal affairs with the excuse of human rights and is against the politicization of the human rights issue in the UN Human Rights Commission. In order to enhance international communication, China has published white papers since 1991 to explain to the world the efforts and the progresses China has made in this regard. These white papers include Human Rights Situation in China (1991), China's Progresses in Human Rights (1995), Progress in China's Human Rights Cause in 1996 (1997), Freedom of Religious Belief in China (1997), New Progress in Human Rights in the Tibet Autonomous Region (1998), Fifty Years of Progress in China's Human Rights (2000), Progress in China's Human Rights Causes in 2000 (2001), Progress in China's Human Rights Cause in 2003 (2004), and China's Progress in Human Rights in 2004 (2005).

China has actively conducted bilateral dialogues on human rights with the European Union, Australia, Canada, America, Norway, and other coun-tries. It has been involved in international cooperation on human rights within the framework of the UN, joined 22 international human rights conventions, and signed the Memorandum of Understanding for the Technical Coopera-tion in Human Rights with the UN High Commissioner of Human Rights in November 2000.

China is in favor of and supports the reform of UN human rights bodies for more democracy and transparency. The essence of the reform is the depoliticizing of human rights issues, rejecting double standards, and replacing Cold War mentality with dialogues based on equality and mutual respect. China proposed that human rights issues should be handled in a balanced manner so as to properly handle the relationship between the universal and special aspects of human rights, and that the choices of different countries in protecting and promoting human rights should be respected.

Supporting the UN Reform

In order to better adapt to the changing international situation and increase the efficiency of the UN, China has been actively supporting the UN reform. The Chinese government issued China's Position Paper on UN Reform, which laid out China's policy on UN reform in a systematic and comprehensive way. The paper states: Reform should be in the interests of multilateralism, and enhance the UN's authority and efficiency, as well as its capacity to deal with new threats and challenges. The reform should be all-dimensional and multisectoral, and should aim to succeed in both security and development; especially, the reform

Chinese President Hu Jintao meets with the UN Secretary General Ban Ki-moon in Beijing in July 2008.

should aim at reversing the trend of the "UN giving priority to security over development." The reform shall accommodate the propositions and concerns of all UN members, especially those of developing countries.

On the core issue of UN reform—the reform of the United Nations Security Council—China proposes: The reform of the UN Security Council is multifaceted, encompassing the enlargement of the UN Security Council and the increases in its efficiency. The reform should be conducive to enhancing the authority and efficiency of the Council, and strengthening its capacity to deal with global threats and challenges. Increasing the representation of developing countries should be given priority. The principle of geographic balance should be adhered to, with representation of different cultures and civilizations taken into consideration.

Playing a Responsible Role in the Settlement of Global Issues

As China grows in power and becomes more integrated with the international community, the Chinese government has proactively participated in the coordination and cooperation within the international society, lived up to its obligations, and shared the responsibility of a big power in maintaining world security and promoting global development.

Handling the Global Economic Issues with a Strong Sense of Responsibility

As economic globalization has led to an intimately connected world economy, an economic crisis or recession in any form will have negative repercussions on a global scale. Since its opening up, China's export-oriented economy has made China and the world so intertwined as to make them an inseparable whole. All global economic crises have had great negative impact on the Chinese economy. However, China is convinced that in the era of globalization, China's economy cannot sustain fast development without the development and prosperity of the world economy as well as the rise of its neighbors; and China has realized that helping others is helping itself. When a regional or global economic crisis happens, China is ready to bear the cost, undertake its responsibility, and plays a very positive role. For instance, China found its economy under great pressure when China's Southeast Asian neighbors were struck with a serious financial crisis in 1997. Having surmounted many difficulties, domestically China maintained the stability of its Renminbi and increased its domestic consumption. Internationally China provided large amount of economic aid to those

A group photo of Chinese President Hu Jintao with other leaders attending the 3rd G-20 Financial Summit held in Pittsburgh, USA in September 2009.

Southeast Asian countries seriously hit through bilateral arrangements and the International Monetary Fund. This had helped Southeast Asian countries overcome the crisis and enabled China to win the trust of its neighbors.

Since its participation in the World Trade Organization (WTO) in 2001, China has adhered to the principle of balancing rights and obligations while strictly following the WTO rules to fulfill its obligations. China have lived up to its commitments by lowering tariffs and reducing other trade barriers, revising its domestic laws and regulations, opening up more areas to the outside world, increasing the degree of free trade in commodities, enlarging trade openness in the service sector, stepping up intellectual property rights protection, and increasing transparency in trade policies. Within the WTO, China stands for perfecting the international trade and financial system, promoting free trade and open investment, and the settlement of trade frictions through coordination and cooperation.

The subprime crisis that started in the US in 2008 has caused an international financial crisis, which has produced a far-reaching impact on the world economy and taken a heavy toll on the Chinese economy. In order to cope with the crisis, the Chinese government has swiftly adjusted its macroeconomic policy and formulated a proactive fiscal policy and a moderately loose monetary policy in addition to a stimulus package that aims at driving economic growth through both consumption and investment. Domestically China accelerated investment, giving priority to projects affecting people's well-being, infrastructure, and environmental protection. Globally, China has vigorously participated in international cooperation. It has opposed trade and investment protectionism, calling for countries to maintain confidence, enhance communication, and render mutual support. China has called for the following measures: enhancing and improving the IMF's surveillance over the macro-economic policies of the economies of the major reserve currencies; improving the governing body of the IMF and the World Bank; streamlining the international monetary system so as to enhance surveillance over the issuing and administrating mechanisms of the major reserve currencies; stabilizing exchange rates between the major reserve currencies; and pluralizing and rationalizing the international monetary system. What the Chinese government did has minimized the negative impact of the international financial crisis on China, and contributed to the recovery and growth of the world economy.

International Cooperation on the Global War on Terrorism

The September 11 attack against the US has transformed terrorism from an ordinary nontraditional issue into a public hazard of the world. Taking strict precaution against and opposing terrorism have become major new tasks of national security and strategy facing major countries of the world.

China has been a victim of terrorism. The Eastern Turkistan Islamic Movement and other terrorist groups have carried out terrorist attacks in China's Xinjiang Autonomous Region, resulting in injuries and deaths as well as damage to property, seriously jeopardizing the social stability and the lives and property of the peoples of different ethnic groups in the area. In coping with this public hazard, China has made its policy on anti-terrorism in conformity with the new concept of security featuring "mutual trust, mutual benefit, equality, and coordination" and joined the international efforts in fighting global terrorism.

China holds that the war against terrorism should be conducted in a comprehensive way to address both the root causes and symptoms with a focus on rooting out the causes of terrorism. Fighting terrorism should depend on concrete evidence and have a clear target in conformity with the purpose and principle of the UN Charter and other universally accepted international norms. The United Nations and its Security Council should play a leading role. Terrorism should not be linked to any specific nation or religion and double standards should be avoided in fighting terrorism. The international community should make joint efforts to resolutely condemn and fight terrorism in all forms regardless of their targets, places, and manifestations.

Chinese and foreign servicemen in a joint anti-terrorism military exercise.

China firmly supports and takes part in international anti-terrorism cooperation. China has acceded to the International Convention for the Suppression of Terrorist Bombings and signed the International Convention for the Suppression of the Financing of Terrorism. The country has joined 10 and signed one of the 12 international anti-terror conventions. China and other members of the Shanghai Cooperation Organization signed the Shanghai Convention on the fight against terrorism, separatism, and extremism in 2001.

China has conducted consultations and exchanges on counter-terrorism with the US, Russia, Britain, France, Pakistan, India, and more than 30 other countries, and has actively participated in the UN Security Council's Commission on Fighting Terrorism. At the suggestion of China, the APEC Shanghai Summit Meeting issued a statement on fighting terrorism. In addition, China also prompted the heads of government, ministers of defense, heads of the law-enforcement ministries, as well as foreign ministers of the members of Shanghai Cooperation Organization (SCO) to issue a joint statement on fighting terrorism. It also supported the establishment of a permanent SCO anti-terrorism center to organize joint anti-terrorist military exercises within the framework of the SCO. For example, a Sino-Kyrgyzstani joint anti-terrorist military exercise was conducted in October 2002; a similar exercise was organized in August 2003, involving Kazakhstan, Kirgizstan, and

Russian Tajikistan in China's Xinjiang and Kazakhstan; and a Sino-Russian exercise titled "Cooperation-2007" took place in September 2007, participated by the Chinese military police and the Russian police of the Ministry of Internal Affairs.

Participating in the Programs of International Community in Dealing with Climate Change

Global climate change and its adverse effects are a common concern of mankind. Fully aware of the importance and urgency of addressing climate change and taking into overall consideration both economic development and ecological construction, the Chinese government released in 2007 the China National Plan for Coping with Climate Change, setting its general objectives to be met by 2010.

China has actively participated in the international programs for dealing with climate changes. China adheres to the principle of being "mutually beneficial, pragmatic, and effective" and "common but differentiated in responsibilities" in participating in and promoting international cooperation in the field of climate change. China's president and premier have both stated China's position at multilateral and bilateral exchanges, including the outreach session of the G8 summit, Asia-Pacific Economic Cooperation (APEC) meeting, East Asia Summit (EAS), and Bo'ao Forum for Asia.

China has acceded to more than 50 international treaties or conventions on environment protection, including the United Nations Framework Convention on Climate Change, the Kyoto Protocol, the Montreal Protocol on Substances that Deplete the Ozone Layer, the Stockholm Convention on Persistent Organic Pollutants, the Convention on Biological Diversity, and the United Nations Convention to Combat Desertification.

China energetically cooperates with foreign governments, international organizations, and research institutes in climate change research. It actively participates in international scientific cooperative programs, including the World Climate Research Program (WCRP) under the framework of the Earth System Science Partnership (ESSP), International Geosphere-Biosphere Program (IGBP), Global Climate Observation System (GCOS), Global Ocean Observation System (GOOS), Array for Real-Time Geostrophic Oceanography (ARGO), and the International Polar Year. In addition, China has stepped up its efforts to share information and resource with international organizations and institutions. Up to July 20, 2008, China had 244 cooperative projects under the Clean Development Mechanism (CDM) successfully registered with the United Nations; and these projects were expected to reduce carbon dioxide emissions by 113 million tons annually.

Chinese Foreign Minister Yang Jiechi addresses the UN High-level Meeting on Climate Change in September 2007.

Promoting the Settlement of Regional Hot Issues

After the end of the Cold War, the international situation relaxed in general but regional hot spots and conflicts remain common, jeopardizing regional stability. At the same time, earthquakes, tsunamis, and other natural disasters have frequently caused damages to the human lives and development.

Whenever a country is struck by any natural disaster, the Chinese government has always been ready to provide humanitarian assistance. For instance, when the Indian Ocean earthquake and tsunami caused disastrous consequences in 2004, the Chinese government and people started the biggest foreign assistance campaign since the founding of the PRC by providing timely and sincere assistance to the tsunami-hit countries for disaster relief and reconstruction. In the settlement of regional hot spots, the Chinese government has followed international principles, and spoken out for justice by playing a constructive role.

On the Middle East Issue

The Middle East issue or the conflicts between Arab countries, including Palestine, and Israel have brought the two sides to three large-scale wars since 1947, making nearly one million Palestinians homeless. The conflicts between Arabs and Israelis have been escalating, making it the longest regional hot issue in the world.

China has always been sympathetic to the misfortunes of the Palestinian people and has resolutely supported the struggle of Arabic and Palestinian people to recover their lost land and restore their national right. As early as 1988, China recognized the State of Palestine and established diplomatic ties with it. On the other hand, China does not oppose the Jewish nation or the Israeli people, and does not support the idea of dismantling the state of Israel.

The history and reality of the Middle East has shown that military force cannot solve the issue, and confrontation is detrimental to the settlement of

The UN Meeting for Asia and the Pacific on the Question of Palestine is held in Beijing in December 2003.

the issue. China has supported the Middle East peace process, dispatched its special envoy for Middle East affairs, and made its efforts and due contribution to the progress in the Middle East peace process. China holds that the relevant UN resolutions on the Middle East issue and the "land for peace" principle set in the Madrid peace conference have provided a basis for Middle East peace talks. The key to breaking the deadlock in the Middle East peace talks is that the parties concerned should faithfully implement the agreements and understandings that have been reached. China has held that the parties concerned should settle the Jerusalem issue, the crux and most difficult part of the Middle East issue, through negotiation based on the relevant UN resolutions; and unilateral actions that go against the settlement of the issue should be avoided.

On the Afghanistan Issue

Afghanistan is China's close neighbor and one of the first few countries that established diplomatic ties with China. As the only Afghan neighbor that does not have any unsettled issue left over from history with Afghanistan, China has always supported the Afghan people's righteous cause of national liberation and national sovereignty.

After the September 11 Incident in 2001, Afghanistan became the focus of international attention as the focus of the US counter-terrorist war shifted to this country. As a close neighbor of Afghanistan, China hopes that Afghanistan becomes a peaceful country, a country that can cooperate with the international community, and a country where different ethnic groups can live together in peace. China holds that the independence, sovereignty, and territorial integrity of Afghanistan should be respected, and that the Afghan issue should be finally settled by the Afghans themselves. China has supported the effort by the Afghan interim government to encourage the different factions within Afghan to give priority to their country and peace, and maintain peace and stability so as to proceed with their national building. At the same time, China holds the view that the political settlement of the Afghan issue is impossible without the role of the UN. China supports the efforts of the UN toward the peaceful settlement of the Afghan issue, and supports the United Nations Assistance Mission in Afghanistan to play a leading and coordinating role in the process of Afghan reconstruction.

China has vigorously supported the efforts of the Afghan government and people in maintaining stability in their country, developing their economy, and national reconstruction. China has rendered aid to Afghanistan in the forms of material, cash, and preferential loans, and has joined the international community to push forward Afghan reconstruction and promote peace and stability

An agreement is signed in Beijing in January 2002 on assistance of the Chinese government to the Interim Government of Afghanistan.

by participating in the construction of such infrastructure as roads, water conservancies, and hospitals.

On the Issue of Darfur in Sudan

Due to drought and desertification in the western part of Sudan, conflicts and competition for water and grassland between different tribes began to occur in the 1960s and 1970s, leading to the deterioration in the regional situation and culminating in large-scale conflicts between the anti-government troops and the government forces, making Darfur a hot spot attracting the attention of the international community.

China has advocated that the sovereignty and territorial integrity of Sudan should be respected and the Darfur issue should be settled through political means by equal dialogue and consultation. Pressures or sanctions, or threatening with force, should be avoided. China has held that the measures taken by the United Nations Security Council should reflect the common wishes of the international society, address the legitimate concerns of the Sudanese government, and take the final and proper settlement of the issue as the basis. The international community should help Sudan improve the humanitarian and security situation in Darfur, and provide assistance in reconstruction and development

The second batch of peacekeeping troops of the Chinese PLA to Sudan set out from Xinzheng International Airport, Henan Province on January 16, 2007.

so as to realize peace, stability, and development in the Darfur area as early as possible. While trying to settle the Darfur issue, the international community should give full play to the leading role of the UN-African Union-Sudanese government trilateral mechanism, with a balanced consideration for peacekeeping and the political settlement of the Darfur issue.

Keeping in mind the long-term stability and development of Sudan, China has provided constructive suggestions and advice to the Sudanese government and facilitated communication and coordination between the Sudanese government and related parties. The Chinese government dispatched its special envoy to Darfur in 2007, who paid visits to Sudan and other related countries including those in Europe, America, and Africa, as well as the United Nations, the African Union, the Arab Union, and EU headquarters. China has maintained close contacts with, and persuaded on different occasions, related parties to narrow their differences, increase mutual trust, and reduce suspicion of each other so as to reach an agreement on the deployment of a Joint Mission in Darfur along with the African Union and the United Nations. China, as the chair of the United Nations Security Council in July 2007, pushed the United Nations Security Council to pass resolution 1769 unanimously, attaining a first-phase achievement in the efforts by the international community to settle the Darfur issue. At the request of the United Nations, China promised to send 315 multifunctional engineers to join the peacekeeping mission in Darfur. In addition, China has provided humanitarian aid to Darfur and participated in its reconstruction and development.

On the North Korean Nuclear Issue

The international security environment has undergone tremendous changes following the end of the Cold War. On the one hand, some countries started their efforts to develop nuclear weapons for their own security or other concerns. On the other hand, the proliferation of weapons of mass destruction and their delivery system has become a major worry of and a hot issue in the international community. The nuclear issues in North Korea and Iran are two salient examples.

The North Korean nuclear issue has remained a focus of international concern since the early 1990s. As a close neighbor who has vital interests in the settlement of the North Korean nuclear issue, China has paid close attention

A scene of the six-party (China, the Democratic People's Republic of Korea, the United States, the Republic of Korea, Japan, and Russia) talk on the Korean nuclear issue held in Beijing.

to the issue and vigorously engaged itself in multilateral diplomacy in order to solve the issue. After the issue escalated in 2003, China hosted first the Three-Party Talk (China, North Korea, and the United States) and then the Six-Party Talk (China, the Democratic Republic of Korea, the United States, the Republic of Korea, Russia, and Japan) in Beijing. China has been instrumental in getting the participants to issue the Initial Actions for the Implementation of the Joint Statement in February 2007 and the Second-Phase Actions for the Implementation of the Joint Statement in October 2007. This has set the final goal of a nuclear-free Korean Peninsula.

An opponent of nuclear proliferation, China has advocated the denuclearization of the Korean Peninsula and has made relentless efforts to maintain long-lasting peace and stability in the Peninsula. China expressed its opposition when the Democratic Republic of Korea (DPRK), in defiance of the opposition from the international community, conducted two nuclear tests in October 2006 and May 2009, respectively. China voted for the United Nations Security Council's resolution 1874 on North Korean nuclear tests when the DPRK conducted its second nuclear test, demanding that North Korea stop any activities that would worsen the situation. At the same time, China has held that as a sovereign nation and a member of the United Nations, DPRK should be respected in terms of its sovereignty, territorial integrity, and other legitimate security concerns, as well as its development interests; and that DPRK should enjoy the same right to peaceful use of nuclear technology as other signatories once it returns to the Non-proliferation Treaty. China stands for the peaceful settlement of the North Korean nuclear issue through dialogue and consultation so as to maintain the peace and stability of the Korean Peninsula and Northeast Asia at large.

On the Iran Nuclear Issue

The Iran nuclear issue, which is identical in nature to the North Korean issue, escalated into an international hot one in 2003. Iran has insisted that it is entitled to peaceful use of nuclear technology, but has not been able to maintain a consistent stand in its cooperation with the International Atomic Energy Agency (IAEA) and its suspension of uranium enrichment activities. The West has exerted pressure on Iran's nuclear plan, leading to a deadlock between the two sides over this issue.

China has been in favor of the international nuclear nonproliferation system all along. It maintains that the Iran nuclear issue should be settled by political and diplomatic means so as to maintain peace and stability in the Middle East area; Iran should enjoy the right to peaceful use of nuclear technology. China appreciates Iran's repeated promise that it does not have the plan to develop nuclear weapons and that it is willing to cooperate with the IAEA. China also holds that Iran, a signatory of the Non-proliferation Treaty, should live up to its international commitments, help maintain the international non-proliferation mechanism, and enhance its cooperation with the IAEA as it enjoys the right to the peaceful use of nuclear technology.

China has been actively involved in the process of examining the Iranian nuclear issue in the IAEA and the United Nations Security Council, and has attended the conferences on Iran's nuclear issue that involve the foreign ministers of six countries and the political director-generals from the foreign ministries of the six countries. In April 2008, it hosted the meeting of political director-generals from the foreign ministries of the six countries on the Iranian nuclear issue in Shanghai in order to promote a peaceful settlement of the issue.

Chapter 4

Following the Five Principles of Peaceful Coexistence, and Developing Omnidirectional Diplomacy

Mutual respect for sovereignty and territorial integrity, mutual nonaggression, noninterference in each other's internal affairs, equality and mutual benefit, and peaceful coexistence are important international norms. China's diplomacy has been characterized by developing peaceful and friendly relations with all countries on the basis of these five principles.

China has faithfully adhered to these five principles of peaceful coexistence in developing its relations with different countries of the world. This has stabilized China's relations with the developed countries as a whole, and improved its relations with its neighbors and developing countries, leading to a best ever international and peripheral environment for China since 1949.

The Development of the Five Principles of Peaceful Coexistence

The Five Principles of Peaceful Coexistence was first proposed by Chinese Premier Zhou Enlai when meeting with an Indian delegation visiting China in December 1943 to negotiate with its Chinese counterpart on questions concerning their relations with Tibet of China. Premier Zhou proposed in his talk: "Immediately after its birth, New China has set its principles on handling its relations with India, namely: mutual respect for territorial integrity, mutual nonaggression, noninterference in each other's internal affairs, equality and

Chinese Premier Zhou Enlai reiterates the Five Principles of Peaceful Coexistence at the Asian-African Conference held in Bandung, Indonesia in April 1955.

mutual benefit, and peaceful coexistence." The Indian side agreed with these principles, which were later included in the Preamble to the Agreement between the People's Republic of China and the Republic of India on Trade and Intercourse Between the Tibet Region of China and India.

The Chinese delegation led by Zhou Enlai participated in the Asian-African (Bandung) Conference attended by 29 countries from Asia and Africa, which was held in Bandung, Indonesia in April 1955. The 10 principles on international relations adopted in the final communiqué of the conference is an extension of the Five Principles of Peaceful Coexistence. Thereafter, China settled the boundary issues that were left over from history with Burma, Mongolia, Pakistan, and Afghanistan, consecutively, on the basis of these principles.

In his tour to 14 countries in Asia, Africa, and Europe from the end of 1963 to early 1964, Zhou Enlai put forward eight principles on China's economic and technical aid to foreign countries, which extended the Five Principles of Peaceful Coexistence to the field of international economic cooperation. Many international instruments, including the Joint Communiqué between the People's Republic of China and the United States of America (also referred to as the Shanghai Communiqué) reached between the two governments when American President Nixon visited China in 1972, the Joint Communiqué on the Establishment of Diplomatic Relations between the People's Republic of China and the United States of America in 1978, as well as the Sino-Japanese Treaty of Peace and Friendship signed by the two governments in 1978, have all emphasized the Five Principles of Peaceful Coexistence as the guiding principles in developing bilateral relations.

The five principles were put forward initially to guide China's relations with countries with different social systems. However, later historical experiences have shown that if the principles are followed, countries with different social systems can live in harmony and maintain amicable cooperation, not just countries with similar social systems.

China is not only an advocator but also a practitioner of the Five Principles of Peaceful Coexistence. So far the Five Principles have been incorporated in the communiquéés or other important bilateral instruments between China and 171 countries. China sticks to them in establishing and developing

Chinese Premier Zhou Enlai meets Kliment Yefremovich Voroshilov, Chairman of the Presidium of the Supreme Soviet in Moscow during his visit to the Soviet Union, Poland, and Hungary in January 1957. During the visit Premier Zhou stressed that the socialist countries should also observe the Five Principles of Peaceful Coexistence.

relations with all countries of the world and aims to build a peaceful, stable, fair, and reasonable international political and economic order.

Maintaining Stable and Peaceful Relations with Developed Countries

Diplomacy is an important instrument for countries to further their foreign policy goals and to safeguard their national interests. National interests are multidimensional and vary from time to time due to different circumstances. In the first 30 years after the founding of the PRC, the priority of China's national interests was to safeguard national sovereignty, territorial integrity, and security. With the shift from political to economic issues domestically, the priority of China's national interests since the 1980s changed to that of promoting China's economic development, increasing China's comprehensive national strength, and improving the living standards of the Chinese people. Consequently, the major task of China's diplomacy moved to creating an international environment of lasting peace and a favorable climate in China's periphery for domestic economic development.

An international seminar is held in Beijing in June 2004 to mark the 50th anniversary of the birth of the Five Principles of Peaceful Coexistence. Attending the seminar were more than 100 statesmen and scholars of 13 countries from five continents.

In light of China's current foreign-policy goal, it is of special significance to maintain a stable relationship with the developed countries. From the perspective of keeping China's economic development, major developed countries, namely, the United States, European Union, and Japan, are China's major trade partners. According to Chinese statistics, China's trade with these three economies accounted for more than 40 percent of China's total trade volume in the last few years, and their investment in China amounted to a quarter of China's total foreign investment. In addition, they are also the major sources of China's high-tech imports and the major destinations of Chinese students going abroad to further their education. Maintaining a stable relationship with developed countries has been one of China's successful diplomatic stories since its reform and opening up, and also a precondition for China to continue its sustained economic development domestically.

From a political and security perspective, China has a political system, value system, and lifestyle that are different from those of the developed countries, and many of the political and security problems that China faces today have something, more or less, to do with them. Moreover, the bilateral relations between China and these countries can impact China's relations with other countries, and in the long run will determine whether China will be able to attain its diplomatic goal. For all these reasons, the Chinese government pays great importance to its relations with developed countries.

Sino-American relations

China's relations with the United States is the most crucial one among China's relations with all the Western powers. China is the biggest developing country, and the US the biggest developed country. Therefore, Sino-US relations are important not only for the two countries but for the world as a whole. Having experienced 60 years of difficulties and hardships, including confrontations and frictions as well as cooperation and coordination, the two sides have formed a highly interdependent relationship through enhanced communication.

In retrospect, the 60 years of Sino-US relations can be divided into three 20-year periods. The first 20 years after New China's founding witnessed Sino-US rivalry, confrontation, and conflicts. The US refused to recognize the government of the PRC, and pursued a China policy of political isolation, economic embargo, and military containment. To safeguard its hard-won sovereignty, independence, and territorial integrity, the Chinese government had to engage in full-scale struggles with the US.

The second 20-year period was one of Sino-US strategic cooperation. The changing balance of power between the US and the Soviet Union in the late 1960s not only changed international structure, but helped bring about the Sino-US rapprochement. China and the US released the Shanghai Communiqué during President Nixon's visit to China in 1972, which not only opened the door for Sino-US diplomatic normalization but also started the process of bilateral strategic cooperation. The realization of bilateral diplomatic relations in 1979 ushered China and the US into a new era of cooperation in areas such as strategy, economy and trade, education, and culture.

Sino-US relations entered their third 20-year period of turmoil, adjustment, and adaptation after the end of the Cold War. The turmoil started when the US imposed sanctions on China in 1989. The US government, disregarding its commitments on reducing arms sales to Taiwan, made a decision to sell Taiwan fighter planes worth US$6 billion in 1992. It again contradicted itself by allowing Lee Teng-hui, then Taiwan leader and an advocator of "Taiwan independence," to visit the US in 1995. US-led NATO, while intervening in the internal affairs of former Yugoslavia, bombed the Chinese Embassy there in 1999. In 2001, the US government increased its air surveillance on China, leading to a collision between an American spy plane and a Chinese fighter plane near Chinese territory, resulting in the destruction of the Chinese plane and the death of its pilot. All these infringements upon Chinese sovereignty by the US caused strong opposition and protest from the Chinese people and the Chinese government, and Sino-US relations suffered repeated setbacks.

Differences do remain between China and the US under the current situation. However, their common interests have been on the rise and by far surpass their differences. China and the US have common interests on a large array of issues, including maintaining world peace; settling global and regional issues, such as the prevention of weapons of mass destruction; settling the nuclear issue in Korean Peninsula and Iran; cracking down on transnational crimes; coping with climate change and natural disaster relief; and controlling the spread of infectious diseases. Enhanced communication and cooperation over these issues has become the new basis of bilateral strategic cooperation.

Chairman Mao Zedong and Premier Zhou Enlai talk with US President Richard Nixon and his National Security advisor Dr. Henry Kissinger in February 1972.

Chinese leader, Deng Xiaoping, at a welcoming ceremony at the White House hosted by US President Jimmy Carter in January 1979. Deng was the first Chinese leader to visit the United States since the founding of the People's Republic of China in 1949.

Fast-growing economic and trade relations have become a new catalyst for Sino-US relations. The volume of bilateral trade, which was US$2.4 billion in 1979 when the Sino-US diplomatic relations were normalized, exceeded US$300 billion in 2008. The two countries are now each other's second-largest trading partner. In addition to economic and trade cooperation, contacts and exchanges between China and the United States at different levels are becoming ever more frequent, and the two countries have put in place more than 60 dialogue and consultation mechanisms in six major categories, covering political relations, economy, military, law enforcement, science and technology, education, energy, environmental protection, aviation, and so on. Moreover, bilateral relations are no longer restricted to the relationship between the two states or the two governments. Rather they have expanded to bilateral relations between the two societies and the two peoples.

Chinese President Jiang Zemin and US President Bill Clinton at an event during President Jiang's visit to the United States in October–November 1997.

For instance, people-to-people exchanges, which were scarce when the bilateral relations were first normalized, reached 2.1 million person/times every year. The two sides have 35 sister provinces/states and 145 sister cities. All these have bound China and the US together.

Differences and frictions increased as bilateral ties were enhanced, and Taiwan remains the most sensitive and crucial issue between China and the US. In spite of China's consistent opposition, the US has insisted on selling weapons to Taiwan, and upgraded its substantial relations with Taiwan. These have all encroached upon China's sovereignty, interfered with China's internal affairs, and undermined China's core national interests. Besides, the US has often made use of the Tibet, human rights, religious, and other issues that are purely domestic in nature to interfere in China's internal affairs. Such US policies are detrimental to the overall Sino-US cooperation and are strongly opposed by the Chinese government.

China values the Sino-US relations and hopes that the relations develop stably and smoothly on the principles enshrined in the three bilateral joint communiqués. The two countries agreed on a joint effort to build constructive and cooperative China-US relations during the first meeting between Chinese President Hu Jintao and American President Barack Obama when they participated in the G-20 financial summit held in London in April 2009. To implement this consensus, the two sides have launched a mechanism of Sino-American Strategic and Economic Dialogue, which has become an important platform for the two sides to expand consensus, reduce differences, deepen mutual trust, and promote cooperation.

Chinese President Hu Jintao meets with US President George Bush during the dialogue between G8 and developing countries held in Hokkaido, Japan in July 2008.

Chinese President Hu Jintao meets with US President Barak Obama during the G20 financial summit held in London in April 2009.

Sino-EU relations

China is the biggest developing country, while Europe is an area that has the most developed countries. European Union (EU) is the biggest economic group made up of developed countries. Sino-EU relations are one of the most important bilateral relations for China, and China's consistent policy has been to develop close relations with the EU.

Constrained by the Cold War structure, France was the only Western European country that had established diplomatic relations with China by 1964. The rest of Europe didn't start diplomatic relations with China until the 1970s as the international situation relaxed, and China established formal ties with the EU (known as European Economic Community at that time) in 1975. At present, China maintains diplomatic relations with all European countries but the Vatican.

With its foreign policy adjusted in the early 1980s, China has advanced a policy of developing relations with other countries regardless of their political system or ideologies. This made it possible to develop relations with Western Europe, Canada, Australia, and New Zealand, who are complementary in

Leaders of China and the European Union meet for their 6th summit in Beijing in October 2003. Attending the meeting were Chinese Premier Wen Jiabao, European Council Chairman and Italian Prime Minister Silvio Berlusconi, and the President of the Commission of European Union Romano Prodi.

economic fields, but with different political systems. High-level visits started, and trade volume increased quickly due to various forms of cooperation in different fields. Under such favorable conditions, China reached agreements with Great Britain and Portugal, respectively, on the principles concerning China's resumption of exercising sovereignty over Hong Kong and Macau.

Sino-EU relations experienced a setback in 1989, but returned to normal not long after. The British and Italian Prime Ministers paid consecutive visits to China in 1991, while Chinese President Jiang Zemin paid an official state visit to France in 1994, during which he put forward China's principles on developing relations with countries in Western Europe. And in the same year, the EU lifted all but arms embargoes on China that were imposed in 1989. Rapid progresses have been made ever since. In 1998, China and EU agreed to establish a mechanism of annual summits. In 2001, the two sides agreed to establish a comprehensive partnership, which was promoted to a comprehensive strategic partnership in 2003. So far, China and the EU have established 50 mechanisms of consultation and dialogues covering such fields as politics, economic and trade, science, energy, and environmental protection.

Sino-EU relations are of global strategic significance. China has always valued the role and influence of the EU in regional and international affairs, and welcomed the EU playing a constructive role in international affairs. China has always supported European integration. China's EU Policy Paper, issued by the Chinese government in October 2003, elaborates on the EU's position in China's overall foreign relations, and reflected China's determination to upgrade the Sino-EU relations to a long-term stable and comprehensive partnership. The document also puts forward China's EU policy goals, and details China's concrete ideas on strengthening Sino-EU relations in the field of politics, economic, education, science, culture, social, legal, administration, and the military.

The EU also attaches great importance to its relations with China and welcomes China's opening up and development. It supports China to continue its road of peaceful development. The EU passed A Long Term Policy on EU-China Relations in 1995, defining the strategic framework of the EU-China policy. Since then, the EU has consecutively issued the following policy papers to elaborate the guidelines, goals, and principles behind the EU-China policy: the EU's New Strategy in Cooperation with China (1996), Building a Comprehensive Partnership with China (1998), the EU's China Strategy: the Implementation of 1998 Document and More Effective Steps to Promote the EU's Policy in the Future (2001), and A Maturing Partnership: Shared Interests and Challenges in EU-China relations (2003).

Sound Sino-EU political relations have paved the way for bilateral economic relations. The EU became China's largest trade partner in 2004, after its

Chinese Premier Wen Jiabao and President of the Commission of European Union José Manuel Barroso meet the press after their meeting in China in April 2008.

eastward expansion. The two-way trade reached US$425.6 billion in 2008, making the EU not only China's biggest trade partner, but China's largest exporting market and largest source of technical imports, and the fourth largest source of foreign investments. Almost all the big enterprises in the EU have investments in China.

The progress in Sino-EU relations by no means implies that bilateral relations have not encountered difficulties. Among all the differences and difficulties that pose the greatest harm to the bilateral relations are those that concern China's territorial and sovereignty integrity. For instance, the Netherlands government's insistence on selling Taiwan submarines in 1982, despite China's strong opposition, led to the degrading of Sino-Dutch relations. The French government's decision to sell Taiwan Mirage-2000 fighters in 1992 caused a major setback in their bilateral relations. Recent examples include the disturbances with the Beijing Olympic torch relay in its Europe leg, particularly the Paris leg, and the French leader's insistence on meeting with the Dalai Lama. All reversed the development of Sino-EU relations. Furthermore, as bilateral relations deepen, economic frictions become common occurrences in bilateral relations.

China and the EU do not have conflict in their respective fundamental interests, nor does their comprehensive partnership demand that the two sides should agree on every issue. The two sides need to reduce differences, deepen mutual trust, and broaden the scope of their cooperation on the basis of seeking common ground while reserving differences.

Relations with Japan

Japan and China are neighboring countries with a long history of friendship, separated only by a strip of water. Japan waged wars against China before the founding of the PRC and caused great sufferings to the Chinese people. Referring to this unpleasant historical episode, the late Chinese Premier Zhou Enlai remarked: "(The Sino-Japanese relations are) 2,000 years of friendship, punctuated by only 50 years of confrontation." And he put forward the following principle for developing bilateral relations: "Learning from history and facing up to the future."

Thanks to the shifts in the international structure in the 1970s, China and Japan put an end to their abnormal relations and established diplomatic ties in 1972. According to the provisions of the Sino-Japanese Joint Statement for normalizing bilateral relations, the two sides signed the Sino-Japanese Treaty of Peace and Friendship in 1978, which laid the political foundation for the good neighborly relationship between China and Japan.

Great progress has been achieved in Sino-Japanese relations since the 1980s. High-level visits have been frequent, and bilateral cooperative mechanisms at different levels have been established, such as the Joint Cabinet Member

Chinese Premier Zhou Enlai and Japanese Prime Minister Kakuei Tanaka exchange signed copies of the China-Japan Joint Statement in Beijing in September 1972.

Conference, the Sino-Japanese Friendship Committee of 21st Century formed by senior, junior, and young generation members from the two sides, the Regular Consultation between the Two Foreign Ministries, and Sino-Japanese Security Consultation.

Sound development of political relations has created a favorable environment for Sino-Japanese cooperation in economy, trade, and other areas. The Chinese government declared in the Sino-Japanese Joint Statement that: "in the interest of the friendship between the Chinese and the Japanese peoples, it (China) renounces its demand for war reparation from Japan." On the Japanese side, it has provided four packages of government yen loans to China amounting to 2.65 trillion Japanese yen from 1979 to 2000. Bilateral trade reached US$266.79 billion in 2008, making Japan China's third-largest partner, second-largest foreign investor, and China Japan's largest trade partner. The fast-growing Chinese economy has brought about important opportunities for Japan, making China an important external driving force for Japan's economic recovery.

Discordant notes remain in Sino-Japanese relations. The biggest disturbance concerns how the Japanese government views its history of aggression. In the Joint Statement that marked the normalization of bilateral relations, the

The China-Japan Treaty of Peace and Friendship is signed in Beijing in August 1978.

Chinese Premier Wen Jiabao holds a welcome ceremony at the Great Hall of the People for visiting Japanese Prime Minister Yasuo Fukuda on December 28, 2007.

Japanese side admitted that it "is keenly conscious of the responsibility for the serious damages that Japan caused in the past to the Chinese people through war, and deeply reproaches itself." However, the Japanese government, since the 1980s, has "examined and approved" some school history textbooks that distorted and whitewashed the history of aggression, and has caused protests from China and Japan's other Asian neighbors. In 1985, the Japanese Prime Minister paid homage in his official capacity to the Yasukuni Shrine where 14 class A World War II criminals were worshiped. This was protested by China and other Asian countries, and since then, Japanese leaders have stopped visiting the shrine. But at the beginning of the 21st century, the Japanese leader once again disregarded the opposition from Chinese and other Asian peoples and insisted on visiting the shrine in the name of prime minister, leading to the suspension of high-level visits between China and Japan.

The Taiwan question is another factor hindering Sino-Japanese relations. Taiwan was under Japanese colonial rule for 50 years and was returned to China in accordance with the relevant international documents. The Sino-Japanese Joint Statement provides: "The government of the People's Republic of China reiterates that Taiwan is an inalienable part of the territory of the People's Republic of China. The government of Japan fully understands and

Japanese Emperor Akihito holds a welcome ceremony at the Japanese Court for Chinese President Hu Jintao during his visit to Japan on May 7, 2008.

respects this stand of the government of the People's Republic of China, and it firmly maintains its stand under Article 8 of the Potsdam Proclamation." However, some Japanese politicians continued to interfere in the Taiwan issue. China has made its policy unambiguously clear that it does not oppose Japan having nonofficial relations with Taiwan, but it is strongly against Japan having any official relations with Taiwan that would lead to "two Chinas" or "One China, One Taiwan" in any form.

In consideration of the concerns expressed by China and other countries that had been invaded by Japan in the past, the new Japanese leaders stopped paying homage to the Yasukuni Shrine in October 2006, removing the major obstacle in the Sino-Japanese relations. Prime Minister Shinzo Abe paid an official visit to China, which was called an "icebreaking visit" in 2006. In April 2007, Chinese Premier Wen Jiabao returned an "ice-melting visit" to Japan, during which the two parties issued a Sino-Japanese Joint Communiqué that reaffirms the two sides' efforts to develop a bilateral "strategic relationship of mutual benefit," putting bilateral relations on the normal track. Japanese Prime Minister Yasuo Fukuda's "meeting the spring" visit to China in May 2008 and Chinese President Hu Jintao's "warm spring" visit to Japan demonstrated that Sino-Japanese relations are now on a normal track.

Good Sino-Japanese relations are beneficial to the two nations. China is ready to develop Sino-Japanese relations based on peaceful coexistence and mutual benefit and is committed to attaining common development for generations to come in accordance with the principles enshrined in the Sino-Japanese Joint Declaration and other political documents.

Strengthening Good Neighborly Relations

The Chinese idiom—The teeth will be exposed to the cold once the lips are gone—well demonstrates the history and summarizes the experiences of China's relations with its neighbors. "Neighbors are dearer than relatives from far away" is the firsthand experiences in developing relations with its neighbors.

Many of China's neighbors gained independence from Western colonial rule around the time when the PRC was founded, marking a new starting point for China's relations with its neighbors. While settling the issues left over from history with India, China put forward the Five Principles of Peaceful Coexistence, and jointly proposed to the world these principles together with India and Burma. Based on the principle of equality and mutual benefit, China has settled boundary issues left over from history consecutively with Burma, Nepal, Afghanistan, Mongolia, and Korea, making most parts of China's borders friendly and peaceful.

Since its reform and opening up, China's diplomacy has focused on creating a good peripheral environment for its domestic economic development, and China has made relentless efforts to develop good neighborly relations with its peripheral countries. China's traditional friendships with its neighbors have been cemented, and its relations with ASEAN, Mongolia, Vietnam, India, and other neighbors have been gradually improved.

After the end of the Cold War, China settled most of the boundary issues with its neighbors in the spirit of equal consultation, mutual understanding and accommodation, or reached consensus to shelve them pending their final solution. China has successively reached agreements with India, Pakistan, Nepal, and ASEAN to build bilateral partnerships of different kinds since 1996.

The progress and steady development in its relations with Russia, China's biggest neighbor, is a model of China's success in establishing good neighborly relations. Sino-Russian relations developed from the Sino-Soviet relations. The Soviet Union was the first country that recognized the PRC and established

China and Burma conclude an agreement and a treaty on boundary issues in Beijing in 1960. This was the first time New China and a neighboring country solved their past border issues.

Chinese and Vietnamese officials sign an agreement on border trade. In November 1991, General Secretary Do Muoi of the Vietnamese Communist Party visited China and the two counties normalized their relations.

diplomatic ties with the PRC upon its founding, and Sino-Soviet relations witnessed friendly alliance in the 1950s, deterioration and confrontation in the 1960s and 1970s, and rapprochement and normalization in the 1980s.

The Soviet Union disintegrated on December 26, 1991, shortly after the normalization of Sino-Soviet relations in 1989. As Russia inherited the legal

Chinese President Hu Jintao meets with visiting Russian President Vladimir Putin in October 2004.

status of the Soviet Union on the international stage, Sino-Soviet relations gave way smoothly to peaceful Sino-Russian relations. The two sides agreed in December 1992 to deepen their bilateral relations on the basis of the UN Charter, the Five Principles of Peaceful Coexistence, and other recognized principles of international laws. The leaders of the two countries frequently exchange views on international or regional issues of common concern in their regular visits to each other's countries, in the UN, and at the Shanghai Cooperation Organization (Shanghai Five) summits, promoting their bilateral relations from "constructive partnership" to "constructive strategic partnership" and finally to "partnership of strategic coordination based on equality and mutual benefit and oriented toward the 21st century." The two heads of state signed in 2001 the Treaty of Good Neighborliness and Friendly Cooperation between the People's Republic of China and the Russian Federation, which reiterated that the two sides would continue to develop their good-neighborly, friendly, strategic partnership of cooperation based on equality and mutual trust. The treaty also codifies the idea that the two countries and the two peoples will carry on the "friendly relations from generation to generation, and never become enemies."

China has advanced the concept of creating a secure, amicable, and prosperous neighborhood, and tried to build a good neighborly relationship and

Chinese President Hu Jintao and Russian President Dmitry A. Medvedev sign a Joint Statement of the People's Republic of China and the Russian Federation on Major International Issues in Beijing on May 23, 2008.

partnership with its neighbors in the 21st century. China has helped resolve hot spots, and participated in or facilitated the formation of the regional multilateral mechanism. These foreign policy efforts have helped create a win-win peripheral environment based on peace, stability, equality and mutual trust, and cooperation.

The good peripheral neighborly relations are manifested first in China's relations with Southeast Asian countries. The Chinese government's policy during the Asian financial crisis in 1997 and its stand toward the remaining boundary disputes with certain countries brought about a change in the perception of Southeast countries toward China. In the political realm, China has enhanced mutual trust with ASEAN members by actively participating in the ASEAN Regional Forum (ARF), and has reached agreements through multilateral dialogue and cooperation, including the Declaration on the Conduct of Parties in the South China Sea, the Joint Declaration of ASEAN and China on Cooperation in the Field of Non-Traditional Security Issues, and the Treaty of Amity and Cooperation in Southeast Asia in 2003.

In the economic realm, bilateral trade and economic relations between China and ASEAN members have been forcefully strengthened through the

Chinese President Jiang Zemin attends the informal meeting of leaders of ASEAN plus China, Japan, and the Republic of Korea in Kuala Lumpur, Malaysia in December 1997.

A summit commemorating the 15th anniversary of ASEAN-China dialogue relations is held in Nanning, Guangxi Zhuang Autonomous Region in November 2006.

Chinese Premier Wen Jiabao and Indian Prime Minister Atal Behari Vajpayee exchange signed copies of the Declaration on Principles for Relations and Comprehensive Cooperation between the People's Republic of China and the Republic of India during Prime Minister Vajpayee's official visit to China in June 2003.

cooperative framework of ASEAN plus China, Japan, and South Korea (10+3), and ASEAN plus China (10+1). China and ASEAN signed the Framework Agreement on Comprehensive Economic Cooperation between ASEAN and the People's Republic of China in 2002, laying out plans for establishing a China-ASEAN trade zone by 2010. After the implementation of Trade in Goods Agreement between China and ASEAN in 2005, more than 7,000 kinds of goods began to enjoy tariff reduction, and this has further boosted the bilateral trade.

Second are China's relations with Northwestern neighbors. The heads of state from China, Russia, Kazakhstan, Kyrgyzstan, and Tajikistan met in Shanghai and Moscow in 1996 and 1997, respectively, reaching agreements on strengthening mutual confidence in the military fields and disarmament in the border regions. These meetings launched the annual meeting mechanism of the Shanghai Five, which not only facilitated the peaceful settlement of outstanding boundary issues between them, but also increased mutual trust among member states. In addition, the sphere of mutual benefit and cooperation was expanded to include security, politics, diplomacy, economy, and culture.

The fruitful cooperation among the Shanghai Five led to the establishment of the Shanghai Cooperation Organization (SCO) in 2001. Since its inception, the SCO has pursued the Shanghai spirit of mutual trust, mutual benefit, and

Chinese President Hu Jintao and Pakistani President Pervez Musharraf are to sign the Joint Declaration of the People's Republic of China and the Islamic Republic of Pakistan on the Directions of Bilateral Cooperation in Beijing in November 2003.

equality, as well as respecting the diversity of civilizations and seeking common development. China and the SCO members have followed the principle of nonalignment, inclusiveness, and not targeting other countries or regions. Due to its growing, the SCO, which originally consisted of China, Russia, Kazakhstan, Kyrgyzstan, Tajikistan, and Uzbekistan, has admitted Mongolia, Pakistan, Iran, and India as observers, and Sri Lanka and Belo Russia as dialogue partners. SCO has become an important platform for maintaining regional security in China's northwestern border and increasing mutual trust among its members.

Third are its relations with southwestern neighbors. The frequent visits between Chinese and Indian and Pakistani leaders have led to improved Sino-Indian relations and the consolidated traditional friendship between China and Pakistan. The leaders of China and India confirmed in 2000 the forging of a strategic partnership in the 21st century, and the two sides further signed the Joint Declaration on Principles for Relations and Comprehensive Cooperation in 2003, agreeing to maintain the status quo pending the final resolution of Sino-Indian boundary issue. At the same time, the two sides agreed to designate their respective representatives to explore the framework for the final settlement of the boundary issues. Sino-Indian relations have shown a good momentum as bilateral political trust deepens, and cooperation has expanded in the field of trade and economy, defense, as

Chinese President Hu Jintao meets with ROK President Lee Myung-bak and Japanese Prime Minister Yukio Hatoyama before the second China-Japan-ROK trilateral leaders' meeting held in Beijing on October 10, 2009.

well as humanitarian areas. At the same time, the Sino-Pakistani traditional friendship has also been consolidated through proactive mutual beneficial cooperation between the two sides. China's sound relations with both India and Pakistan, two important developing countries with regional influence, have relaxed the tensions in the sub-Asian continent and improved China's northwestern border security.

Last are China's relations with its northeastern neighbors. After the Korean nuclear issue escalated into a crisis, China engaged in a shuttle diplomacy by dispatching its envoys to countries concerned, enabling the six parties— the DPRC, the US, the ROK, Japan, Russia, and China—to come to the negotiation table. During this process, China hosted each round of talks, provided facilities, chaired each session, and motivated the parties to set the ultimate goal of denuclearizing the Korean Peninsula. China insisted that the North Korean nuclear issue should be settled through dialogue and peaceful means to prevent the issue getting out of control. China's diplomatic efforts not only contributed to regional peace, but were conducive to the security of Northeast Asia.

PARTNERSHIPS CHINA HAS ESTABLISHED WITH ITS NEIGHBORS SINCE THE 1990S

- In 1994, Constructive Partnership with Russia
- In 1996, Constructive Partnership Oriented to the 21st Century with India
- In 1996, Comprehensive Partnership Oriented to the 21st Century with Pakistan
- In 1996, Partnership for Generations Oriented to the 21st Century with Nepal
- In 1997, Good-Neighborly Partnership of Mutual Trust Oriented to the 21st Century with ASEAN
- In 1998, Partnership of Friendship and Cooperation for Peace and Development with Japan
- In 1998, Cooperative Partnership Oriented to the 21st Century with ROK
- In 2003, China Strategic Partnership for Peace and Prosperity with ASEAN
- In 2003, Good-Neighborly Partnership of Mutual Trust with Mongolia
- In 2005, Peace- and Prosperity-Oriented Strategic Cooperative Partnership with India
- In 2005, Strategic Partnership with Indonesia
- In 2005, Strategic Partnership with Kazakhstan
- In 2006, Strategic Partnership of Mutual Benefit with Japan
- In 2008, Strategic Cooperative Partnership with ROK

Enhancing Solidarity and Cooperation with Other Developing Countries

Developing countries mainly concentrate in Asia, Africa, and Latin America, and most of them have similar historical sufferings, situations, and desires to China, which provide a solid basis for good bilateral relations between China and other developing countries.

China's relations with African and Arab countries

China's relations with African and Arab countries started from the first Asian-African Conference held in Bandung, Indonesia in 1955. Chinese Premier Zhou Enlai put forward at this conference the principle of seeking common ground while putting aside differences, which eliminated the worries and misunderstandings of some developing countries about China. China established diplomatic ties with Egypt in 1956, a significant start in its relations with African and Arab countries. To date, China has established diplomatic ties with all Arab countries and 48 of the 53 African countries.

China and the majority of the African and Arab countries have been supportive of each other all along. China has firmly supported their desire to uphold national independence and pursue national economic development. During his visit to 10 Asian and African countries from December 1963 to February 1964, Premier Zhou Enlai put forward five principles for guiding China's relations with African and Arab countries and eight principles on China's aid to African countries. The Tanzara Railway constructed with a 988-million-yuan, interest-free loan from the Chinese government is a monument of friendship between China and Africa.

African countries had firmly supported China in its bid to restore its lawful seat in the UN. Twenty-six of the 76 countries that voted in the 26th session

Malian President Modibo Kaita greets Chinese Premier Zhou Enlai at the airport of Mali in January 1964. From October 1963 to February 1964 Premier Zhou and Vice-Premier Chen Yi visited 13 countries in Asia and Africa. The 13-nation tour was a landmark in China's friendly relations with Asia-African countries.

of the UN General Assembly in 1971 for the resolution to restore China's legitimate rights in the UN were from Africa. The late Chairman Mao Zedong noted that: "it is our African friends who have brought us back to the United Nations."

Since China has had its legitimate rights in the UN restored, it has stood firmly by the side of developing countries. For instance, China voted 16 times in succession in order for the candidate Salim Ahmed Salim, Tanzanian Foreign Minister, to be elected UN Secretary-General in 1982. Although Salim failed to be elected as anticipated, the new Secretary-General, Javier Perez de Cuellar, was also from a developing country. In 1991, China worked energetically to support African countries in the election of the UN Secretary-General, leading to the election of Boutros-Ghali, Egyptian vice Prime Minister, as the Secretary-General of the United Nations.

China has made it the cornerstone and starting point of its foreign relations to strengthen solidarity and cooperation with other developing countries since its reform and opening up, and has endeavored to explore new ways and means to promote mutually beneficial bilateral cooperation with other developing countries. China has supported and actively participated in South-South

The Tanzania-Zambia Railway, a well-known project in China's program of foreign assistance. Construction of the 1,860-km railway started in October 1970 and was completed in July 1976.

cooperation, and advanced four principles on expanding economic and trade ties with developing countries, namely, equality and mutual benefit, stress on practical results, diversity in form, and attainment of common progress. As an important part of China's opening-up policy, the cooperation between China and other developing countries has been substantiated in content and expanded in scale, forming a situation of win-win cooperation.

Further progress has been made in Sino-African relations since the end of the Cold War. Nine heads of state from sub-Saharan African countries visited China in 1989 alone. During his visit to six African countries in 1996, Chinese President Jiang Zemin put forward a five-point proposal for the development of a 21st century-oriented, long-term, stable China-Africa relationship of all-around cooperation: to treat each other as equals, develop sincere friendship, strengthen solidarity and cooperation, and seek common development.

To jointly meet the challenges in the new century, China, motivated by some African countries, proposed the establishment of the Forum on China-Africa Cooperation, which has become a new platform to strengthen

Chinese Foreign Minister Li Zhaoxing and Secretary General Amre Moussa of the League of Arab States announce the establishment of the Forum on China-Arab Cooperation at a press conference in Cairo, Egypt, on January 13, 2004.

Sino-Africa consultation and cooperation. At the first Ministerial Conference of the Forum held in October 2001, China announced the cancellation of 10 billion yuan of debts owed by the heavily indebted poor countries and least developed countries in Africa, and to provide special funds to support and encourage Chinese enterprises to carry out mutually beneficial cooperation in Africa. The Forum on China-Africa Cooperation-Addis Ababa Action Plan (2004–2006,) issued at the second Ministerial Conference of the Forum in 2003, and the Declaration of the Beijing Summit of the Forum on China-Africa Cooperation and the Beijing Action Plan of the Forum on China-Africa Cooperation (2007–2009), adopted at the third Ministerial Conference and the first summit held in Beijing in 2006, all promoted and deepened China-Africa cooperation. After the eight commitments on aiding African countries proposed at the Beijing summit in 2006 had been fully implemented, the Chinese government made another eight promises on aiding Africa at the fourth ministerial conference of the forum held in Egypt in November 2009. China's policies have won extensive acclaim from African countries and praise from the international community.

Chinese President Hu Jintao, Ethiopian Prime Minister Meles Zenawi, and Egyptian President Hosni Mubarak jointly read out the Declaration of the Beijing Summit of the Forum on China-Africa Cooperation (FOCAC) held in Beijing in November 2006.

Mutually beneficial and win-win economic cooperation between China and Africa has witnessed steady growth in the 21st century. China-Africa trade volume enjoyed a robust boost from over US$10 million in 1950 to US$106.8 billion in 2008, making China the third-largest trade partner of Africa. China's investments in Africa covered 49 African countries, injecting strong impetus to local economic development.

The Chinese government issued China's African Policy Paper in 2006, which called for the establishment of a new type of strategic partnership between China and Africa, featuring political equality and mutual trust, win-win economic cooperation, and cultural exchanges. The paper also elaborated on the aims and means of China's African policy, and laid out plans for bilateral cooperation in various fields in the future.

The Sino-Arabic Forum was founded in 2004 following the success of the Forum on China-Africa Cooperation. The forum has become a new mechanism to strengthen Sino-Arabic dialogue and cooperation. Under this mechanism, China and Arab countries adopted vigorous measures to promote bilateral exchanges and cooperation in such fields as economy and trade, investment, energy, education, culture, science and technology, public health, and environment, so as to attain common development of the two sides.

Chinese Primer Wen Jiabao addresses the 4th Ministerial Conference of the Forum on China-Africa Cooperation held in Sharm el-Sheikh in November 2009.

EIGHT MEASURES TO STRENGTHEN CHINA-AFRICA COOPERATION ANNOUNCED BY THE CHINESE GOVERNMENT IN 2009

1. Establishing a China-Africa partnership to address climate change and build 100 clean energy projects for Africa.
2. Enhancing cooperation in science and technology by launching a China-Africa science and technology partnership, under which China will carry out 100 joint projects with Africa and receive 100 African post-doctoral fellows.
3. Helping Africa build up financing capacity, providing US$10 billion in concessional loans to African countries.
4. Further opening up its market to African products by implementing, in phases, zero-tariff on 95 percent of the products from the least developed African countries and starting with 60 percent of the products within 2010.
5. Further enhancing cooperation with Africa in agriculture, increasing the number of its agricultural technology demonstration centers in Africa to 20, and training 2,000 agricultural technology personnel for Africa.
6. Deepening cooperation in medical care and health, providing medical equipment and anti-malaria materials worth 500 million yuan (US$73.2 million), and training 3,000 doctors and nurses for Africa.
7. Enhancing cooperation in human resources development and education, building 50 schools and training 1,500 school principals and teachers for African countries, increasing the number of Chinese government scholarships to Africa to 5,500 and training 20,000 professionals for Africa by 2012.
8. Expanding people-to-people and cultural exchanges by launching a China-Africa joint research and exchange program to increase exchanges and cooperation.

China's relations with Latin American countries

China and Latin American countries are all developing countries. Due to the long distance between them and the differences in their natural conditions, social systems, and cultural traditions, New China started developing its relations with Latin American countries later than with other regions. However, the relations have developed very fast thus far, and now have become an important part of China's external relations.

Latin America has traditionally been referred to as the "backyard" of the US. Except for Sino-Cuban diplomatic relations, which were normalized in 1960, no breakthrough was made in China's relations with the rest of the Latin American countries until Sino-US relations were normalized in the early 1970s when 11 Latin American countries established diplomatic relations with China consecutively.

Strengthening solidarity and cooperation with other developing countries, including Latin American countries, has been the cornerstone of China's foreign relations since its reform and opening up. The head of the Chinese government paid a first visit to Latin America in 1985, proposing four guidelines for China's relations with Latin America, namely, peace and friendship, mutual support, equality and mutual benefit, and attainment of common progress. During this visit, as many as 15 agreements, cooperating on politics, economy, trade, science and technology, culture, and financial issues, were concluded between China and Columbia, Brazil, Argentina, and Venezuela, laying a solid foundation for China's friendly relations with Latin American countries in various fields. Since then, Sino-Latin American relations have entered a new period of comprehensive development that include both inter-governmental and people-to-people cooperation.

Acceleration of globalization since the end of the Cold War has shortened the distance between China and Latin American countries, and Sino-Latin American relations were further strengthened. Chinese President Jiang Zemin paid a visit to Mexico in 1997, and six countries—Chile, Argentina, Uruguay, Cuba, Venezuela, and Brazil—in 2001. From 1996 to 2004, eight presidents, three governors, and three premiers from Latin America paid friendly visits to China. Visits of top leaders from the two sides have greatly consolidated bilateral cooperation between China and Latin American countries.

The 21st century has witnessed the new development in the relations between China and Latin America, featuring continuous exchanges of high-level visits, strengthened political ties, and new progress in economic and trade cooperation. President Hu Jintao paid visits to Brazil, Argentina, Chile, and Cuba in 2004 and Costa Rica, Cuba, and Peru in 2008. The Chinese Foreign Ministry issued China's Policy Paper on Latin America and the Caribbean in

Chinese President Jiang Zemin delivers a speech on China-Latin America friendship and cooperation at the UN Economic Commission for Latin America and the Caribbean (ECLAC) during his tour of six Latin American countries in April 2001.

2008, which elaborated the goal and fields of cooperation in China's relations with Latin America, put forward the guiding principle for Sino-Latin American cooperation, and laid a more solid foundation for the comprehensive development of Sino-Latin American relations.

At present, China has maintained diplomatic ties with 21 of the 33 Latin American countries. Since its establishment of a "strategic partnership" with Brazil in 1993, China has set up a "strategic partnership for future common development" with Venezuela, a "strategic partnership" with Mexico, Argentina, and Peru, and a "strategic partnership of common development" with Chile. The political consultation between China and Latin American countries has been further institutionalized and the dialogue mechanisms have been improved.

China has also worked together with Latin America in the multilateral arena. It became an observer in Inter-America Development Bank and in Latin American Integration Association in 1991 and 1993, respectively. Thereafter, China became an observer in the Organization of American States and the UN Economic Commission for Latin America, successively, in 2000 and 2004. In addition, China has also launched dialogue mechanisms with the Rio Group, Southern African Development Community (SADC), and the Andean Group, and established foreign ministerial consultation mechanisms with major Latin American countries.

Chinese President Hu Jintao delivers a speech "Building Comprehensive Cooperative Partnership between China and Latin America in the New Era" at the Peruvian Congress in November 2008.

Strong political relations create favorable conditions for economic and trade cooperation between China and major Latin American countries. China has signed agreements on economic and/or technological cooperation with 16 Latin American countries, and has reached agreements on investment promotion and mutual investment protection with 11 countries. Treaties on avoiding double taxation were also concluded between China and five Latin American countries. All of these instruments have facilitated the remarkable progress in Sino-Latin American economic and trade cooperation. For instance, the trade volume between China and Latin American countries was only US$1 billion in 1979. That volume reached US$143.3 billion in 2008, making China the third-largest trade partner of Latin America.

Sino-Latin American economic and trade cooperation continues to develop in various fields on an increasingly solid foundation. The role of Latin American countries in China's foreign relations is on the rise and will become more and more important in the future.

Chapter 5

Adapting to Globalization, and Promoting Comprehensive Diplomacy

Globalization is a comprehensive and multilevel process. In the economic sphere, almost all countries have chosen the market economy as their mode of economic development regardless of their different social systems and development status. International trade and global investment have expanded at an unprecedented rate in both geographical distribution and scale, making the world an intertwined global market.

In the process of economic globalization, new means of communication based on high technology has not only shortened the distance between countries and regions, but also provided the material foundation for the globalization of production and market, and brought about information globalization. Meanwhile, the extensive employment of modern transportation has made long-distance travel possible within a short time, and cross-border migration is on the rise. The world we live in has become a global village.

Globalization has intimately connected countries and made them interdependent. It has not only changed the relationship between internal and external affairs, and blurred their boundaries, but also changed the environment, issues, methods, and means, and even the content and concept of diplomacy. Diplomatic agendas are becoming increasingly pluralized, expanding from the conventional political and military realms to that of economy and culture. The subjects of diplomacy have expanded from sovereign state actors to encompass international organizations, transnational corporations, as well as political parties, parliaments, and nongovernmental organizations. Changes are also taking place with diplomatic means and channels.

China regards globalization neither as "a panacea for all development problems" or "a scourge inevitably leading to disaster." Instead, it is "a trend of

China officially joins the World Trade Organization (WTO) in December 2001. This is a sign that China has formally become an important part of the international economic system.

world economic development independent of man's will, and no country can bypass it." No nation would be able to develop its economy in isolation. In light of its national conditions, China has put forward a scientific outlook featuring people-oriented, all-around, coordinated and sustainable development. In foreign affairs, China has unswervingly adhered to the opening-up policy and actively participated in international economic cooperation and competition in conformity with the development of globalization. It has brought forth the concept of "grand diplomacy" or "comprehensive diplomacy" in foreign affairs, which covers multiple areas, levels, and channels.

Broadened Diplomatic Arena

Promoting Economic Diplomacy

The third plenary session of the 11th CPC Central Committee in 1978 decided to shift the focus of domestic work to economic development. Thereafter, the relationship between internal and external affairs reversed the original concept that domestic affairs serve foreign policy goals, making foreign policy serve domestic affairs by creating a sound international and neighboring environment for domestic economic development. With regard to the relationship between politics and economics, "politics in command" gave way to the idea that politics should serve the economy and equal importance is given to politics and economy. The significance of China's economic diplomacy emerged.

As the reform and opening up gathered momentum, China made efforts to promote foreign trade, expand international cooperation, and revise domestic laws to encourage foreign investment and introduce advanced technology. China's seats in the World Bank and International Monetary Fund (IMF) were restored; it joined the Asian Development Bank, and it began to apply for the restoration of its seat in General Agreement on Tariffs and Trade (GATT). These economic activities increased China's openness and strengthened its closer ties with the world, which significantly boosted the country's economic growth and strength. China's economic diplomacy has resulted in remarkable achievement.

Economic globalization continued to surge ahead after the end of the Cold War, presenting China with unprecedented challenges and opportunities in its cause of reform and opening up as well as its modernization drive. The Chinese government realized that prosperity could be sought only if it followed the trend through vigorous participation in the international community. China stepped up the process to integrate into the international economic system,

The 3rd annual meeting of the New Champions of the World Economic Forum is held in Dalian, Liaoning Province in September 2009.

joined APEC, and applied to enter the WTO and other international multi-lateral economic organizations. The idea of economic diplomacy has become more explicit.

The significance of economic diplomacy was further upgraded in China's overall foreign relations since the turn of the 21st century and has drawn much attention from decision-makers. Economic diplomacy has been incorporated into the overall strategy of national economic and social development and embodied in China's omnidirectional foreign relations structure. It has become an effective way to promote China's national interests and an important platform to enhance China's relations with different countries.

First of all, promoting economic diplomacy has been done by cementing China's economic ties, seeking cooperation and avoiding confrontation, and stabilizing the bilateral relations with Western countries so as to ensure the necessary market for China's economic development. Mutually beneficial cooperation on an equal footing in the economic field and rising bilateral trade volumes have become the hallmark of China's relations with the EU, the United States, and Japan.

Secondly, economic diplomacy has become the important means by which China has strengthened its relations with other developing countries. The Chinese government held a national conference on China's economic diplomacy toward developing countries in 2004. The conference emphasized that China should "combine friendly relations and mutual trust in the political field with cooperation and exchanges in the economic field to promote economic ties through political means, and coordinate economic and political relations." It also emphasized that "economic cooperation should be carried out in a diverse manner with a focus on practical effect, and combine trade with investment, and foreign aid funds with credit funds, as well as the strategy of 'going out' with 'inviting in.'" With adjusted policies and new means to enhance bilateral relations, the basis of China's relations with other developing countries has shifted from cooperation in anti-imperialism, anti-colonialism, and striving for and safeguarding national independence, to mutually beneficial economic cooperation.

Thirdly, another major aspect of China's economic diplomacy has been its integration with the global economic mechanisms and participation in global economic cooperation. China submitted its application for the restoration of its GATT contracting status in 1986 and it took the country 17 years of constant effort before it obtained final accession to WTO in October 2001. During the process, China speeded up domestic reforms on the one hand and insisted on the principle of balancing rights and obligations in its negotiation with the WTO China group on the other hand. Since its accession to WTO, China has taken a series of measures to further open up to the outside world within the WTO framework, such as further reducing tariff and non-tariff barriers, promoting liberalization, facilitating trade and investment, strengthening openness in service trade, enhancing transparency in trade, protecting intellectual property rights, and deepening reform in exchange rate formation mechanisms to strengthen the elasticity of the RMB exchange rate. In addition to active participation in the WTO, China has also actively joined other regional and bilateral trade arrangements to create a favorable external environment for the sustained and rapid growth of its economy.

Fourth, China has been vigorously engaged in multilateral economic dialogues and developing free-trade zones with other countries. Chinese leaders have exchanged views with leaders of other countries and personages from the business circle to reach a better understanding, and have facilitated some important cooperative projects through active participation in such international conferences as APEC meetings and World Economic Forum. China has concluded six agreements on establishing free-trade zones with ASEAN and other countries and regions, and is in the process of negotiation with more countries and regions on similar agreements. The number of countries that have recognized China's full-market economy status has climbed to 77. In light of the agreement reached by China and the ASEAN in 2002, the China-ASEAN area will become the world's third-largest free trade area only next to NAFTA and the European Union. Furthermore, since its first participation in the G8 dialogue meeting with major developing countries in 2003, China has kept in close touch with the G8. China has elaborated its views on such important issues as energy and the environment, and played a constructive role in solving global economic problems.

Fifth, in conformity with the ever-changing situation of the world economy, international cooperation in such fields as energy, climate change, and environment has become the new focus in China's economic diplomacy. The Chinese government has attached great importance to global climate change facing mankind. The Chinese government has set up a national working group to tackle the problem of climate change, energy saving, and pollution reduction, and has formulated the National Program on Tackling Climate Change. On the international platform, China has been working harder to promote international cooperation on climate change and has called on developed countries to extend financial and technological support to developing countries in their effort to address climate change.

On the energy issue, China has proposed that cooperation should take the place of competition, and advocated full cooperation among countries in the spirit of mutual benefit to create a win-win or all-win scenario. The Eleventh Five-Year Plan (2007–2012) of China's economic and social development approved in 2006 states explicitly that China will increase its overseas cooperation in oil and gas exploitation on the basis of equality and mutual benefit. China should ensure a safe supply of energy by actively engaging in the international energy system and making full use of the international market.

Building on the experiences of other countries, China has followed a mode that prioritizes friendly political relations and emphasizes economic and trade relations. It has also supplied economic aid and other means to guarantee a stable and viable energy supply for China's domestic economic progress by establishing comprehensive cooperative partnership with energy-producing countries.

Since its reform and opening up, China has used economic diplomacy to maintain stable relations with big powers; substantiate China's relations with other developing countries; ensure the resources, markets, and capitals for China's domestic economic development; and efficiently promote sustained fast growth within China's economy. China's economic diplomacy will further expand in content, and will play an increasingly crucial role in the country's overall diplomacy structure with the changing situation.

Carrying out Cultural Diplomacy

Among all ancient civilizations of the world, the Chinese civilization has experienced no major interruption. External cultural exchanges have been a long tradition in Chinese history. Examples like Zhang Qian's (?–114) epic journey to the Western Regions in the Han Dynasty, Xuan Zang's (602–664) travel to India, Jian Zhen's (688–763) sailing to Japan, and Zheng He's (1371–1433) voyages to the West Seas were all of great historical significance.

Cultural diplomacy refers to conducting diplomatic civilities by sovereign states to further national cultural interests or to achieve national foreign strategy by virtue of cultural exchanges under the guidance of certain cultural policies. The emergence of this concept reflects that international cultural exchanges have moved from the conventional realm of low politics to that of high politics under globalization.

The purpose of diplomacy is to further national interests, first and foremost to safeguard national sovereignty, territorial integrity, and national security. In this regard, the primary purpose of cultural diplomacy is also to safeguard national security. But the major and more concrete goal is to put external cultural exchanges in the framework of government policy to form a favorable national image conducive to the country's overall national foreign policy.

Foreign cultural exchanges play a key part in China's foreign relations. Constrained by the Cold War structure, China's external cultural interaction was once mainly confined to socialist countries led by the Soviet Union and countries friendly to China in Asia, Africa, and Latin America. China and France established diplomatic ties in 1964 and in 1965 the two governments signed a cultural exchange program for the period 1965–1966. This was China's first intergovernmental cultural exchange program with a Western European country. It was stipulated in the Constitution, approved by the fifth session of the Fifth NPC in 1982, to conduct cultural exchanges with other countries, providing a legal assurance for ever-expanding cultural interactions. The strategy of cultural development has been included in China's national development strategies and cultural diplomacy has been recognized as being as important as political diplomacy and economic diplomacy since the turn of the 21st century.

It is important to maintain Chinese cultural security in the context of globalization by consolidating the root of its traditional culture through the revival of Chinese culture and the protection of cultural heritage. In recent years, the Chinese government has taken measures to support public cultural projects, construct cultural facilities, and carry out various types of public cultural activities. Measures have also been taken in the restoration, preservation, and innovation of traditional culture, especially national folk culture.

The rejuvenation and development of Chinese culture could not be achieved without benefiting from all that is best in human civilization. In the process of opening up, China has been open-minded to absorb all the fine achievements of other cultures through drawing on others' strengths and virtues. China's cultural opening-up has been well indicated by the duration of foreign language fever in China, and the increasing popularity among Chinese people of Italian opera, Broadway musicals, the Russian ballet and circus, German symphony, and French painting exhibitions.

Domestic cultural preservation and revitalization pave the way for the promotion of cultural diplomacy. The ideas and theories of China's contemporary diplomacy result mainly from Chinese traditional culture. China strives to uphold coexistence among various civilizations instead of conflict, dialogue instead of confrontation, interaction instead of isolation, and inclusion instead of exclusion. China also strives to learn from others for common prosperity, all of which are deeply rooted in such thoughts of Chinese traditional culture as "Harmony is the most precious," "The gentleman aims at harmony, but not at uniformity, while the mean man seeks uniformity rather than harmony," "Mean what you say and honor your words with real action," and "Don't do unto others what you don't want others to do unto you."

External cultural exchanges are the most direct channel and means of cultural diplomacy. In recent years, China's cultural diplomacy has been

A Chinese Culture Festival held in Washington D.C., US in September 2008.

highlighted by numerous foreign cultural interactions led by the Chinese government. By June 2009, China had set up 96 cultural offices in embassies and consulates in 82 countries, concluded intergovernmental agreements on cultural cooperation and nearly 800 annual cultural exchange programs with 145 countries, and maintained close contact with hundreds of international cultural organizations. Recently China has cooperated with many countries in holding Culture Weeks, Culture Tours, Culture Festivals, and Culture Years on a reciprocal terms to present the charms of profound Chinese culture.

Language is the carrier of culture. Chinese has become one of the world's important languages with the advancement in China's status. Currently, there are more than 30 million people studying Chinese abroad at different levels in various educational institutions that offer Chinese language courses in approximately 100 countries. At present, more than 330 higher education institutions in China offer courses that teach Chinese as a foreign language.

An effective way to help the world understand China is by delivering Chinese culture through the establishment of the Confucius Institute. By 2008, China had funded 256 Confucius Institutes and 58 Confucius classrooms in 81countries since the first Confucius Institute overseas was founded in Seoul, South Korea in 2004. In addition, more than 150 schools and institutions in more than 40 countries have applied to set up a Confucius Institute to date. More and more people in the world are now having the chance to learn and

The founding ceremony of Confucius Institute at George Mason University.

understand Chinese culture by attending Confucius Institutes and Confucius classrooms.

The 2008 Olympic Games provided an excellent platform for displaying Chinese culture to the world. The opening and closing ceremonies that caught worldwide attention, as well as various cultural activities during the Olympic Games, have been good opportunities for other peoples to know and understand Chinese culture. The 2010 World Expo in Shanghai will be another occasion for China to conduct cultural diplomacy and seek exchanges and cooperation with the rest of the world.

The Chinese government has been keen on creating conditions to facilitate nongovernmental cultural exchanges and encouraging cultural enterprises to go global. Sustained and in-depth cultural diplomacy has increased mutual trust between China and its neighbors, strengthened mutual understanding between China and Western developed countries, stabilized and consolidated the traditional friendships between China and developing countries, and enhanced the relationship between China and the countries with whom China does not have diplomatic relations.

Conducting Diplomacy for the People and Protecting the Lawful Rights and Interests of Chinese Nationals and Corporations Overseas

Conducting diplomacy for the people and protecting the lawful rights and interests of Chinese nationals and corporations overseas are an important part of China's diplomacy. Protecting the lawful interests and rights of Chinese nationals abroad is an important task of China's diplomatic departments as well as an important component of China's diplomatic works, which is professionally referred to as consular protection. The Chinese government puts great importance on developing consular relations with other countries. It stands for properly addressing the problems that may arise in bilateral consular relations through equal dialogue and friendly consultations with due consideration accorded to the concerns of each side so as to protect the legitimate rights and interests of their citizens and state, and promote consular relations affairs as well as friendships among countries.

The rise in cross-border movement of people and migration is an important manifestation of globalization. With China's further involvement in the international community, more and more Chinese citizens go abroad for various purposes, ranging from travel, business investment, study, and labor export. In 2008, more than 40 million outbound visits were made by Chinese people and more than 10,000 overseas Chinese-funded organizations were set up in more than 160 countries and regions. The complex international security situation and the growing nontraditional security threats put Chinese nationals and Chinese-funded organizations overseas under great risks, leading to more frequent cases of consular protection.

China's diplomacy takes it as its responsibility to protect the interests of Chinese nationals and corporations overseas. The Chinese government uses nationality as a condition of consular protection, and holds that each country should protect the lawful rights and interests of its own country and citizens in accordance with international law, bilateral treaties, and laws of the country concerned; foreign nationals residing in its territory and those foreign nationals who have violated the local laws should enjoy the rights stipulated by the above laws and treaties regardless of their nationality, race, religion, or political or economic reasons. No countries should shield their nationals who commit offences. China is ready to cooperate in the area of consular protection with countries with which it does not have diplomatic relations.

The Ministry of Foreign Affairs has applied modern technology to disseminate early warnings in consular protection. New columns were added to the official website of the Foreign Ministry to report recent cases occurring in consular protection. Along with the issuance of Guidelines on Proper Behavior for Chinese Citizens in Outbound Travel and Guidelines on Chinese Overseas Consular Protection and Service, the website has also updated its travel advice, and provided tips on traveling to specific countries and regions, especially unsafe areas.

To ensure the smooth undertaking of consular protection, the Chinese government has upgraded and expanded its consular department. Early in 1955, the Department of Consular Affairs was set up under the Chinese Foreign Ministry to take charge of consular protection. With the ever-increasing work of consular protection, the Consular Protection Division of the Department of Consular Affairs was upgraded to Consular Protection Center in 2007. More resources and staff were deployed. As a result, China has more than 240 foreign-service institutions overseas, among which 70 or so specialize in consular affairs, focusing on the protection of the interests of Chinese citizens overseas.

To meet the needs of the changing situation, China's foreign affairs departments have also set up cross-sector coordination mechanisms and emergency response mechanisms. When Chinese citizens or corporations fall victim to accidents and suffer great losses overseas, an emergency response team will be established immediately to formulate work plans, set up hotlines, and collect information. Nowadays, China's foreign-service departments handle more than 30,000 cases of consular protection cases each year.

Developing Military Diplomacy

It is said that diplomacy starts where war ends, indicating that military and diplomatic activities lie not in one sack. But in practice, the military is always associated with diplomacy, and military exchanges make up one major means of enhancing mutual confidence and maintaining peace in times of peace.

China's military diplomacy was featured by "lean to one side," the diplomatic strategy of the PRC in the wake of its founding, with its external relations confined to those with the Soviet Union and other socialist countries in Eastern Europe. During the 1960s and 1970s, the principal means of China's military diplomacy were providing military assistance or training to countries in the Third World in support of their national independence and national liberation movement.

As China's relations with the West have improved since the 1980s, the Chinese armed forces have enhanced and expanded its relations with more countries. The White Paper on China's National Defense, issued by the Chinese government in 1998, put forward the policy of developing omnidirectional and multilevel military diplomacy. The foreign relations of the PLA have

The generals from the Chinese navy and American navy chat over a banquet. The Chinese navy fleet visited Pearl Harbor, Hawaii in September 2006.

experienced historic shifts from the dominance of friendly contacts at the high level to one of pragmatic cooperation in multilevel and wide-ranging patterns, from the dominance of bilateral contacts to equal stress on both bilateral contacts and multilateral contacts, and from contacts between military professionals to omnidirectional foreign contacts.

Implementing the nation's independent foreign policy of peace and its national defense policy that is purely defensive in nature, China's military diplomacy comprises military exchanges with other countries on the Five Principles of Peaceful Coexistence, with the purpose of broadening military relations and deepening military cooperation with other countries. It includes the following major aspects.

First, institutionalizing the mechanism of military communication. By 2008, China had established military ties with more than 150 countries, and had military attache offices in 109 countries. A total of 98 countries have military attache offices in China.

Second, developing high-level military exchanges. Exchange of military visits at the high level is a major form of military diplomacy. From 2007 to 2008, senior PLA delegations visited more than 40 countries, and the defense ministers and chiefs of the general staff from more than 60 countries visited China during the same period.

Third, conducting military cooperation and exchanges in personnel development. From 2007 to 2008, China sent more than 900 military students to more than 30 countries, while 20 military educational institutions in China have established and maintained inter-collegiate exchange relations with their counterparts in more than 20 countries, including the United States, Russia, Japan, and Pakistan. Meanwhile, some 4,000 military personnel from more than 130 countries have come to China to study at Chinese military educational institutions.

Fourth, establishing mechanisms of different types in security cooperative dialogue. China has placed great emphasis on defense consultation and security dialogue with other countries. Today, China has established consultation mechanisms on defense and security with such countries as the United States, Russia, Japan, Australia, Britain, and France. And China has also developed military ties for security with such neighboring countries as Pakistan, India, Mongolia, Thailand, Vietnam, and the Philippines.

Fifth, promoting and participating in regional security cooperation. China, in 1997, participated in the ASEAN Regional Forum (ARF), the only official security and cooperation forum in the Asian-Pacific region. China hosted the first security policy meeting of the ARF in 2004, filling a gap in the dialogue of senior defense officers within the framework of ARF. In recent years, the Chinese armed forces have participated in such dialogue mechanisms as the West Pacific Naval Forum and Shangri-la dialogue session, and conducted effective exchanges and cooperation in the fields of antiterrorism, disaster relief, peacekeeping, maritime security, and joint patrols in border areas.

The Chinese navy fleet leaves for the Gulf of Aden and the Somalia Sea area for escorting merchant ships in 2008.

Sixth, promoting military transparency. China has issued a white paper on China's national defense every other year since 1995, and had issued six by 2009, introducing China's national defense policy and the status of China's defense and armed forces. Additionally, China has taken part in the UN's transparency system for military expenditures, and issued white papers on issues concerning security such as arms control and nonproliferation and space policy.

Seventh, holding joint military exercises with other countries. In October 2002, China and Kyrgyzstan took a joint anti-terrorist military exercise in their border area, which was China's first joint military exercise with foreign armed forces. By 2008, China had had 28 major joint military exercises with armed forces of the countries concerned. In addition China had invited foreign military delegations in China and observers of other countries to observe PLA's military drills.

Eighth, participating actively in international peacekeeping operations and international relief and rescue activities. Since the PLA dispatched its military observers to the UN's peacekeeping operations for the first time in 1990, China has sent more than 10,000 person-times of military personnel and police to 24 UN peacekeeping operations by June 2008. In addition, China International Search and Rescue Team, composed mainly of Chinese servicemen, provided disaster relief services to people stricken by the Indian Ocean tsunami, the Katrina hurricane in US, South Asian earthquakes, and mudslides in the Philippines.

Ninth, participating in international escorting missions in the high seas. The Chinese naval fleet has paid more than 30 visits to more than 40 countries. The Chinese naval fleet headed for the Gulf of Aden and the Somali sea area for escorting missions in December 2008, which signified a major step for the Chinese navy in international military cooperation and maintenance of security in international sea areas.

Multilevel Foreign Relations

Summit Diplomacy

Summit diplomacy refers to the diplomatic activities of the heads of the state or government. Its traditional forms include such activities as visits by heads of state or government, summit meetings, correspondence and phone calls between heads of state or government, dispatching envoys or personal representatives abroad, or delivering foreign policy pronouncements in person.

On October 1, 1949, Mao Zedong proclaimed in the Notice of Central People's Government of the People's Republic of China that "our government is the sole legal government representing the people of the People's Republic of China. It is ready to establish diplomatic relations with all foreign governments that are willing to abide by the principles of equality, mutual benefit, and mutual respect for each other's territorial integrity and sovereignty." This could be regarded as PRC's first summit diplomacy.

However, summit diplomacy was not quite active for various reasons. New China's summit diplomacy during the Cold War was limited to only a few forms, including the issuance of statements and conversations, or visits to other countries made by Chinese heads of state or government or receiving visits by their counterparts. During the 1950s and the 1960s, China's summit diplomacy was restricted to its relations with those countries in Asia, Africa, and Europe that had diplomatic relations with China. For instance, as the chairman of both the Central People's Government and the Communist Party of China, Mao Zedong only made two foreign visits in his lifetime and both were to the Soviet Union.

Since the 1980s, the rapid process of globalization has made summit diplomacy more prominent in international affairs due to these facts: The globalization of international challenges requires leaders from different countries to engage in direct discussions on measures to address them; the media in an age of information globalization has rendered summit diplomacy, especially the summit visits, the focuses or hotspots of the world; summit diplomacy could enable the supreme leaders of countries to engage in face-to-face negotiation so as to efficiently settle the problems they face.

China and the Soviet Union sign the Sino-Soviet Treaty of Friendship, Alliance, and Mutual Assistance during Chairman Mao Zedong's visit to the Soviet Union in February 1950.

Chinese leader Deng Xiaoping meets with Mikhail Gorbachev, Chairman of the Presidium of the Supreme Soviet and General Secretary of the Communist Party of the Soviet Union in May 1989.

The changing international situation has led to proactive summit diplomacy in China. Hotlines have been frequently used for communication between Chinese heads of government and state with their counterparts. Bilateral and multilateral summit conferences have become highlights in the diplomatic arena. Envoy visits have become very popular diplomatic activities. Furthermore, the number of China's summit visits abroad has boomed, covering countries in Asia, Africa, Europe, Oceania, North America, and Latin America. For instance, Jiang Zemin paid visits to more than 70 counties during his term in office from 1989 to 2002 as General Secretary of the CCP and as the president of PRC.

Summit diplomacy has been the major way for China to settle important problems with related countries, and summits have usually been landmark events in China's diplomatic history. At the end of 1949, soon after New China

Chinese President Hu Jintao meets with American President Barak Obama in Beijing in November 2009.

was founded, Chairman Mao Zedong paid a visit to the Soviet Union, and at the beginning of the following year, Premier Zhou Enlai also visited the Soviet Union. These visits were indications of New China's diplomatic strategy of "lean to one side." During Mao's visit, China and the Soviet Union signed the Sino-Soviet Treaty of Friendship, Alliance, and Mutual Assistance, which was of strategic significance for the PRC. Thirty years later, the normalization of Sino-Soviet relations was only realized after the meeting between Chinese leader Deng Xiaoping and Soviet leader Gorbachev. After the disintegration of the Soviet Union, summit diplomacy helped the bilateral relations experience a successful transition from Sino-Soviet relations to Sino-Russian relations.

Summit diplomacy also demonstrates the status of China's relations with different countries. Chinese leaders visited the United States only after the establishment of Sino-US diplomatic relations. The exchanged visits of heads of state and government between China and the US in the mid-1980s manifest the stable bilateral relationship. To the contrary, after the US president imposed sanctions against China in 1989, the exchange of visits at the highest level between the two countries was suspended for nine years. The frequent exchanges of visits by leaders of the two countries reveal the sound Sino-US relations today. For example, President Hu Jintao and President Bush had four

Japanese Emperor Akihito hosts a ceremony welcoming Chinese President Jiang Zemin in November 1998. During this first visit to Japan by China's head of state, the two sides issued the China-Japan Joint Declaration.

meetings and four telephone conversations, and exchanged correspondences 10 times in 2008. Summit diplomacy is not only the symbol of the stable development of Sino-US relations but also provides opportunities to enhance and advance Sino-US relations.

And the same applies to the Sino-Japanese relationship. From 1979 to 1991, the Chinese heads of state and government made five visits to Japan. However, because of the mistaken stance by the Japanese leader at the beginning of the 21st century, China suspended the exchange visits between the two countries, and then the bilateral relationship was trapped in a coexistence of "frosty diplomatic ties and hot economic ties." The exchange visits were not resumed until the new leader of Japan changed the mistaken stance. Such visits as the "ice-breaking journey" by the Japanese prime minister Shinzo Abe to China in April 2006, the "ice-melting trip" by the Chinese premier Wen Jiabao to Japan in 2007, the "early spring journey" by the Japanese premier Yasuo Fukuda to China in December 2007, and the "warm spring journey" by the Chinese president Hu Jintao to Japan in May 2008, indicated that the Sino-Japanese relationship had returned to the right track, and were in the process of being promoted.

Summit diplomacy has functioned as a significant driving force in bilateral relations. The most eye-catching summit visits or meetings are good examples. Each summit visit was accompanied by large political, economic, cultural, and other delegations, which would sign cooperation agreements with their counterparts during the summit visit in the fields of politics, security, trade and economy, energy, education, healthcare, culture, and tourism. The execution of these agreements would become the follow-up harvest of the summit visit, and definitely further promote and substantiate bilateral cooperation. Furthermore, the interpersonal relations between the leaders established during these summit visits would become important ties helping cement bilateral relations, develop long-term bilateral relations, and enhance mutual understanding.

Multilateral summit diplomacy has become a high-profile form of summit diplomacy in today's world and this is also true of China's summit diplomacy. In order to settle such global problems as economic development and environment, China has participated in the global summits conferences held under the framework of the UN. The extended G8 summit with leaders of leading developing countries, and the G20 summit conferences have been frequently held to discuss global economic problems and address economic crises. Many other summit meetings with some regional and trans-regional multilateral organizations have also been held, such as the Shanghai Cooperation Organization, ASEAN-China, East Asian Summit among Japan and South Korea, Asian and Pacific Economic Cooperation (APEC), and Asian-Europe Meeting (ASEM). As leaders of the biggest developing country, China's heads of state and government have taken an active part in these multilateral summit conferences to elaborate China's views and put forward constructive proposals for the settlement of the relevant problems under discussion.

Parliamentary Diplomacy

Parliament is the legislative branch of a state, which occupies an important position in a country's social and political activities. The external relations of the legislative body are an important component of the country's overall foreign relations, playing an exceptional role in enhancing mutual understanding and friendship with other peoples and pushing forward the development of diplomatic relations.

The National People's Congress (NPC) works as the legislative body of the People's Republic of China. The foreign relations of the NPC and its standing committee have always played important roles in each phase of China's social evolution. Since the reform and opening up were initiated, as one important component of China's overall diplomacy, the relations of the NPC with the parliaments of developing countries in Asia, Africa, and Latin America have been deepened, and its relations with the parliaments of Western countries have improved remarkably. China has become increasingly active in multilateral activities of parliament diplomacy and the foreign relations of the NPC have become omnidirectional and multilevel, making NPC an important component of China's overall diplomacy.

The 5th Asia-Europe Parliamentary Partnership Meeting is held in Beijing in June 2008.

Wu Bangguo, the Chairman of the Standing Committee of China's National People's Congress meets with Theo-Ben Gurirab, the president of the Inter-Parliamentary Union (IPU) in Beijing in August 2009.

The foreign relations of the China's NPC have made continuous advancements in recent years. First, the exchanges of visits between the Chinese NPC with its foreign counterparts at different levels have seen a gradual increase. For instance, chairman of the Standing Committee of the NPC, Wu Bangguo, made 10 foreign visits, and members of the meeting of chairmen made 58 foreign visits from 2003 to 2008, covering five continents. During the same period, 109 speakers and vice speakers of foreign parliaments visited China upon invitation.

Second, China's NPC has established quite a few mechanisms of exchanges with foreign parliaments. From 1981, when the first exchange mechanism between NPC and the European Parliament was established, to 2008, the NPC had established exchanges with more than 10 countries' parliaments, including the US House of Representatives and Senate, the Russian Federal Committee and State Duma, Japan's Senate and Diet, South Korea's National Assembly, Indian parliament, the House of Representatives of Australia, Canadian parliament, British parliament, Germany's Bundestag, the French senate, the House of Representatives of Italy, South Africa's National Assembly, the People's Assembly of Egypt, and the House of Representatives of Brazil. In addition, the NPC has set up inter-parliamentary relations with 178 countries, and founded 98 Friendship Groups under the framework of parliament based on the principle of reciprocity.

Third, NPC has actively cooperated with and participated in multilateral affairs of regional or global inter-parliamentary organizations. Up to 2008, NPC had joined 12 international parliament organizations, such as the World Conference of Speakers of Parliaments, Inter-Parliamentary Union, Asian Parliamentary Assembly, the Asian-Pacific Parliamentary Forum, Parlamento Latinoamericano, ASEAN Inter-Parliamentary Organization, and Speakers Conference of Parliaments of Pacific Islands Forum. China is also an observer of three regional parliamentary organizations. China hosted the 12th annual meeting of the Asian-Pacific Parliamentary Forum in Beijing in 2004, and China's NPC hosted the fifth annual Asia-Europe Parliamentary Partnership Meeting in 2008.

Party Diplomacy

The Communist Party of China is the ruling party of China and its foreign relations are an important part of China's overall foreign relations, and are of great significance in promoting China's foreign relations with other countries as well as in maintaining world peace.

The foreign relations of the CCP started before the founding of New China, but they were limited to relations with other Communist parties or worker's parties of the socialist countries in the wake of the PRC's founding due to the international situation.

The 3rd International Conference of Asian Political Parties is held in Beijing in April 2004.

Having drawn experiences and lessons from the history of the party's foreign relations, the 12th CCP National Congress in 1982 began to plan its foreign relations, while separating party-to-party relations from inter-state relations, and put forward the principles of "independence, complete equality, mutual respect, and noninterference in each other's internal affairs" in developing relations with foreign parties.

Thereafter the CCP started extensive contacts and exchanges with different foreign parties. The CCP had established relations with more than 270 foreign parties in more than 110 countries by the end of the Cold War.

Political forces in the world underwent reshuffles and realignments after the end of the Cold War, and parties with different political stances and thoughts were becoming ever more active. In keeping with the developments in the international situation, the CCP has established relations with more foreign parties, with the level of exchanges increased, the content of exchanges substantiated, and areas of the exchanges expanded. By 2008, the CCP had established and maintained friendly relations with 528 parties and political organizations in 166 countries and regions in the world. The CCP conducts dozens of exchanges and visits with its foreign counterparts every year, and these have become important ties to enhance mutual understanding.

Additionally, the CCP has also taken an active part in multilateral activities of international parties. Having participated in the first and second

International Conference of Asian Political Parties, the CCP hosted in Beijing in 2008 the third International Conference of Asian Political Parties, which was attended by leaders and delegates of 81 political parties from 35 countries. The conference has greatly enhanced the mutual understanding between the CCP and other political parties from other Asian countries.

The foreign relations of the CCP have consolidated and enhanced the relationship between the CCP and the ruling parties of socialist countries, enriched the form and substance of its relations with the political parties from developing countries, strengthened its relations with major parties in developed countries, and promoted mutual understanding with the parties of those countries that have not established diplomatic relations with China, creating a favorable situation for the normalization of diplomatic ties between China and these countries.

Enhanced Mutual Understanding by Civil Diplomacy

Civil diplomacy is the conducting of international relations in civil terms, which is different from the diplomacy by government. Put plainly, civil diplomacy is the diplomacy of making friends, which is also referred to as people-to-people diplomacy. It focuses on enhancing trust and understanding between peoples, attaches great importance to communication, and emphasizes establishing friendships that go beyond concrete political and economic interests.

Civil diplomacy has been an important channel to enhance mutual contacts and understanding between countries, and its importance has become prominent against the background of globalization.

China has always put great emphasis on civil diplomacy, and has put forward the ideas of "relying on the people and placing hope on them" in diplomatic practice. In order to enhance the mutual understanding between China and the outside world, the Chinese People's Congress of Defending World Peace, which was merged with the Chinese People's Association for Friendship with Foreign Countries in 1972, and Chinese People's Institute of Foreign Affairs were created in the wake of the founding of New China. China Council for the Promotion of International Trade was founded in 1952 to promote China's trade and economic cooperation with foreign countries. In 1954, these organizations joined hands with more than 10 other nongovernmental organizations, including All China Federation of Trade Unions and All China Women's Federation, to form the Chinese People's Association for Foreign Culture, which was renamed the Chinese People's Association for Friendship with Foreign Countries in 1969. The tradition of civil diplomacy in China has taken shape.

Under the special international circumstances after the founding of New China, civil diplomacy has enhanced mutual understanding between the Chinese people and Japanese people and improved Sino-Japanese relationship by means of "economic ties promoting political ties, and civil ties promoting

Declaration on Promoting Sino-Japanese People's Friendship in the New Century is issued in Beijing in January 2001.

official ties." Civil diplomacy, which has played an indispensable role in facilitating the normalization of Sino-Japanese diplomatic ties, occupies an important position in the history of China's foreign relations.

Since China's reform and opening up, especially in the 21st century, the Chinese People's Association for Friendship with Foreign Countries, the top organization of civil diplomacy in China, has considered the overall situation both home and abroad and set the following guiding policy in developing civil diplomacy: Giving priority to developing civil cooperative relations with great powers—including US, Russia, Japan, and the European Union (group of powers) —and China's neighbors; carrying on civil relations with developing countries; expanding multilateral civil diplomacy with international nongovernmental organizations; and striving to develop civil relations with countries that have not established diplomatic relations with China. The goal of this policy is to create a favorable international and peripheral environment for China's domestic economic development. For instance, when Sino-Japanese relations were trapped in a deadlock at the turn of the 21st century, the Chinese People's Association for Friendship with Foreign Countries and 17 other friendship groups from both China and Japan gathered in Beijing in 2001 to issue the Declaration of Sino-Japanese Civil Friendship in the New Century. In 2005, the Chinese People's Association for Friendship with Foreign Countries hosted another gathering in Tokyo, Japan with participation of 60 friendship groups from the two countries and issued the Appeal for Peace and Good-neighborly Friendship. The civil diplomacy between China and Japan helped

Chinese Vice President Xi Jinping addresses China International Friendship Cities Conference held in Beijing in November 2008.

stabilize bilateral relations, even as exchanges of official visits at the highest level were suspended between the two countries.

The activities between international friendship cities have been another channel and form of civil diplomacy. With the rapid development of China's economy, urbanization in China has been booming. The foreign relations of Chinese cities and other local governments with their foreign counterparts have become an important channel for China's integration with the international community. Since Tianjin of China took the lead in forging a relationship of sister cities with Kobe, Japan in 1973, China had developed 1,500 relationships of sister cities or provinces with 120 countries by 2008. In 1992, the Chinese People's Association for Friendship with Foreign Countries created the China International Friendship Cities Association, which joined the International Union of Local Authorities in 1999. In 2008, China hosted the Congress of International Friendship Cities, attended by more than 500 people from more than 70 provinces and states of over 30 foreign countries as well as more than 50 Chinese cities. The intercity cooperation is growing from bilateral form to multilateral form, and is gradually moving from people-to-people cooperation to covering all the fields, including politics, economy, culture, and society.

Promoting bilateral friendships by setting up bilateral friendship associations is another important form of China's civil diplomacy. In October 1949,

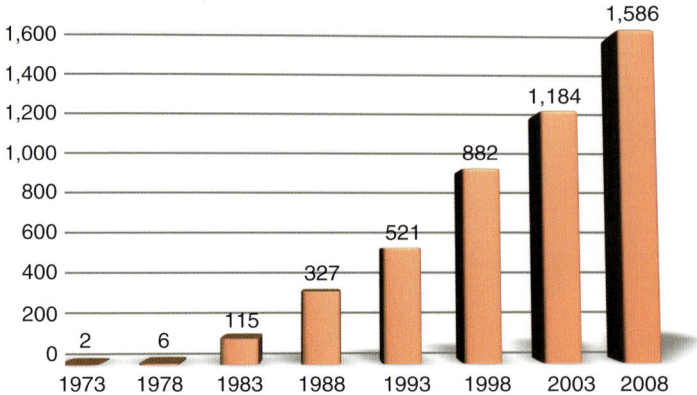

Increase of Friendship Cities between China and Other Countries

China set up the first bilateral friendship association, All China Congress of Sino-Soviet Friendship Association (renamed Sino-Russian Friendship Association in 1992). The Sino-Japanese Friendship Association was founded in 1963. Both of them have played important roles in promoting the Sino-Soviet relationship (Russian) and the Sino-Japanese relationship. Up to 2008, China had established 42 transnational friendship associations, including China-EU Friendship Association, China-Arabian Countries Friendship Association, China-ASEAN Friendship Association, China-Central Asia Friendship Association, and China-US Friendship Association. In addition, China had established friendly cooperation with 458 NGOs in 148 countries, forming a unique network of civil diplomacy that further adds vigor to China's civil diplomacy. Having played an irreplaceable role in the diplomatic history of the PRC, civil diplomacy will continue to enhance the friendship between the Chinese people and the peoples around the world, promoting China's economic and cultural exchanges and cooperation with foreign countries.

Globalization has posed unprecedented challenges for diplomacy today. While coping with these challenges, China has put forward the concept of comprehensive diplomacy, calling for attention to the overall situation while managing foreign affairs. Its main purpose is still to create a favorable international environment for China's domestic economic development, maintain world peace, promote common development, and build a harmonious world of peace and prosperity.

INDEX